Christ's Coming and the World Church

BY GUY DUTY

DIMENSION BOOKS
BETHANY FELLOWSHIP, INC.
Minneapolis, Minnesota

ISBN 0-87123-075-5

DIMENSION BOOKS
are published by
Bethany Fellowship, Inc.
6820 Auto Club Road
Minneapolis, Minnesota 55438

Printed in the United States of America

Preface

Those who read this book will see that I owe much to the work of other authors, and I have given credit to them in places where it is due. However, I may have failed to do this in several places. I especially failed to give favorable mention in chapter 5 to *Trench's Synonyms of the New Testament*.

The reader will also see that I have reached some drastic conclusions from quoted biblical texts. These conclusions may appear harsh but I ask the reader to consider the texts from which they were drawn. I have not meant to be unkind or disrespectful to anyone.

There are many good ministers working to promote a united world church who believe that Jesus is the Son of God and that the Bible is the Word of God. We do not doubt their sincerity in trying to promote world peace and prosperity through ecumenical effort. But if they obey the admonition of Jesus to "watch and pray," they may see the dangers of which Jesus and Paul warned concerning the churches at the end of the age. These dangers have already begun to develop. To Jesus and Paul, world peace and prosperity will be the message and objective of Antichrist to a desperate world.

It often appears to me that some biblical statements are drastic and severe, and the Lord knew they would be offensive to many. He pronounced a blessing upon those who would not be offended at Him and His word.

The apostle John wrote that anyone who does not believe that Jesus is the Christ is "a deceiver and an antichrist." This statement is strong and extreme, and it is true or false. We accept it as true. How then can we cooperate with deceivers and antichrists to promote a world peace which Jesus said He did not come to bring? *"Suppose* ye that I am come to give peace on the earth? I tell you, Nay, but rather division."

The world church peace plan is a denial of God's entire prophetic revelation for the end of the age. And we cannot work for that which the prophecies reveal shall not be.

Jesus spoke of His followers as a "little flock," and He taught that only a comparative "few" would meet His requirements to enter the Kingdom of God. But He said that "many" would go the way of the world. This few-many truth is significant in the teachings of Jesus. Throughout the Scriptures, the Few-Church stands in remarkable contrast to the Many-Church. When Jesus told about His little flock we do not get the idea that He was thinking of earth's millions combined in a world merger of churches whose boast is in their numbers and whose glory is in their popularity.

Paul's theology is different from that found in many systematic theologies. There is much in these theologies that Jesus and Paul did not teach. But they taught the same truths about the few and the many.

Paul drew illustrations of this from Jewish history and he used them as warnings to his Gentile churches. He quoted Isaiah: "Though the number of the children of Israel be as the sand of the sea, [only] a remnant shall be saved." "Even so then at *this present time* also there is a remnant according to the election of grace" (Romans 9:27; 11:5). In these texts *remnant* has the same comparative meaning as *few*.

Note here that "remnant" and "election" are connected. God's purpose of divine election is in the remnant-church. It is not in the multitudes whose number is as "the sand of the sea."

In working out His plan of predestination, God, in all generations, puts the multitudes to the tests of truth and faithfulness. And the results of these tests are the remnants. So, "at this present time also" there is a faithful minority.

We ask our brethren to consider these truths in the light of Christ's coming when we must give account of our lives and works at the judgment-seat.

Guy Duty

CONTENTS

CONTENTS

1

Statement of Purpose

Jesus Christ will return to this earth. Hundreds of prophecies in both Testaments witness to this fact. Angels also gave their testimony to it. At Christ's ascension they told His apostles:

> Ye men of Galilee, why stand ye gazing up into heaven? this same Jesus, which is taken up from you into heaven, shall so come in like manner as ye have seen him go into heaven.—Acts 1:11

The angels gave emphatic repetition to the fact that it will be "this same Jesus" that will come "in like manner." Christ's second coming and the literal manner of it is stressed here. Many teachers say His coming will not be literal but "spiritual." This fallacy is refuted by the language of the angels.

It was in the same exact sense that Jesus promised:

> I will come again and receive you unto myself; that where I am, there ye may be also.
>
> I will see you again, and your heart will rejoice.
> —John 14:3; 16:22

Our subject goes far back in the Genesis history. God gave a vision of Christ's second coming to a man named Enoch. He was so persuaded by this revelation, and so convinced of its reality, that he had the continuous action of faith to walk with God (Heb. 11:5).

And Enoch also, the seventh from Adam, prophesied
. . . saying, Behold, the Lord cometh with ten thousands of his saints,

To execute judgment upon all, and to convince all
that are ungodly among them of all their ungodly
deeds which they have ungodly committed . . .—Jude
14-15

Various details about Christ's coming were added
by succeeding prophets. When God's enemies set
themselves against the Lord and His Anointed at His
coming, God said He will "set my king upon my holy
hill of Zion" (Ps. 2:1-6).

Let's look at a few of the hundreds of prophecies
that describe Christ's return, from Isaiah to Revelation.

And the Redeemer shall come to Zion, and unto
them that turn from transgression in Jacob.—Isa.
59:20

Behold, the days come, saith the Lord, that I will
raise unto David a righteous Branch, and a King
shall reign and prosper, and shall execute judgment
and justice in the earth.

In his days Judah shall be saved, and Israel shall
dwell safely: and this is his name whereby he shall
be called, THE LORD OUR RIGHTEOUSNESS.
—Jer. 23:5-6

I saw in the night visions, and, behold, one like the
Son of man came with the clouds of heaven . . .

And there was given him dominion, and glory, and
a kingdom, that all people, nations, and languages,
should serve him: his dominion is an everlasting
dominion, which shall not pass away, and his kingdom that which shall not be destroyed.—Dan. 7:
13-14

And his feet shall stand in that day upon the mount
of Olives, which is before Jerusalem on the east,
and the mount of Olives shall cleave in the midst
thereof toward the east and toward the west, and

there shall be a very great valley; and half of the mountain shall remove toward the north, and half of it toward the south.—Zech. 14:4

But who may abide the day of his coming? and who shall stand when he appeareth? for he is like a refiner's fire, and like fullers' soap.—Mal. 3:2

John the Baptist preached about Christ's second coming when he said:

Whose fan is in his hand, and he will throughly purge his floor, and gather his wheat into the garner; but he will burn up the chaff with unquenchable fire. —Matt. 3:12

The angel Gabriel referred to Christ's second coming when he told Mary before His birth:

He shall be great and shall be called the Son of the Highest: and the Lord God shall give unto him the throne of his father David:

And he shall reign over the house of Jacob for ever; and of his kingdom there shall be no end.—Luke 1: 32-33

Jesus was the Prophet of all prophets and much of His teaching was prophetic. He gave us more information about His coming than any of the prophets, and He threw light on the subject from many angles. He said:

For as the lightning cometh out of the east, and shineth even unto the west; so shall also the coming of the Son of man be.—Matt. 24:27

Hereafter shall ye see the Son of man sitting on the right hand of power, and coming in the clouds of heaven.—Matt. 26:64

When the Son of man shall come in his glory, and all the holy angels with him, then shall he sit upon the throne of his glory:

And before him shall be gathered all nations: and he shall separate them one from another, as a shepherd divideth his sheep from the goats.—Matt. 25: 31-32

Be ye therefore ready also: for the Son of man cometh at an hour when ye think not.—Luke 12:40

The literal return of Christ is prominent in Paul's epistles. It was a major doctrine in his theology, as we now see:

> For our conversation [citizenship] is in heaven; from whence also we look for the Saviour, the Lord Jesus Christ.—Phil. 3:20

> When Christ, who is our life, shall appear, then shall ye also appear with him in glory.—Col. 3:4

> And the Lord make you to increase and abound in love . . . to the end he may stablish your hearts unblameable in holiness before God, even our Father, at the coming of our Lord Jesus Christ with all his saints.—I Thess. 3:12-13

> Behold, I shew you a mystery: We shall not all sleep, but we shall be changed,

> In a moment, in the twinkling of an eye, at the last trump: for the trumpet shall sound, and the dead shall be raised incorruptible, and we shall be changed.—I Cor. 15:51, 52

> For the Lord himself shall descend from heaven with a shout, with the voice of the archangel, and with the trump of God: and the dead in Christ shall rise first.

> Then we which are alive and remain shall be caught up together with them in the clouds, to meet the Lord in the air: and so shall we ever be with the Lord.—I Thess. 4:16-17

> And the very God of peace sanctify you wholly; and I pray God your whole spirit and soul and body be preserved blameless unto the coming of our Lord Jesus Christ.—I Thess. 5:23

> I charge thee therefore before God, and the Lord Jesus Christ, who shall judge the quick and the dead

at his appearing and his kingdom.—II Tim. 4:1

Looking for that blessed hope, and the glorious appearing of the great God and our Saviour Jesus Christ.—Titus 2:13

Other apostles also wrote about Christ's second coming:

So Christ was once offered to bear the sins of many; and unto them that look for him shall he *appear the second time* without sin unto salvation.—Heb. 9:28. (Note here that to those literal persons that "look for Him," Christ will appear the second time in the same literal sense that He appeared the first time.)

Be patient therefore, brethren, unto the coming of the Lord. Behold, the husbandman waiteth for the precious fruit of the earth, and hath long patience for it, until he [it] receive the early and latter rain.

Be ye also patient; stablish your hearts: for the coming of the Lord draweth nigh.—James 5:7-8

And when the chief Shepherd shall appear, ye shall receive a crown of glory that fadeth not away. —I Pet. 5:4

Beloved, now are we the sons of God, and it doth not yet appear what we shall be: but we know that, when he shall *appear,* we shall be like him; for we shall see him as he is.—I John 3:2

Behold, he cometh with clouds; and every eye shall see him, and they also which pierced him: and all kindreds of the earth shall wail because of him. Even so, Amen.—Rev. 1:7. (Observe that literal peoples of the earth would not wail if they did not see His literal appearance.)

He which testifieth these things saith, Surely I come quickly. Amen. Even so, come, Lord Jesus. —Rev. 22:20

From Enoch to John, the Bible is a message about the coming of Christ, and Revelation closes with a promise and prayer for His return.

The Book of Revelation is a summation of the entire Bible, and it is a fact of vast prophetic importance that there are about 500 Old Testament quotations in Revelation. (These references are listed in *The New Testament in Greek,* Westcott & Hort, New York: Macmillan Co., pp. 612-618, 1953.)

The last four chapters of Revelation describe the final scenes of God's purpose for the creation of the earth and the human race. Some years ago while reading a science magazine, I saw a statement which said that the most unsolved question among philosophers today is this: "Why was the world created?"

We learn from the astronomers that the Milky Way, the galaxy to which our sun belongs, is a family of more than 100 billion stars. And these scientists say there may be as many as 100 billion other galaxies in the universe. And they believe that billions of these stars may have planets and that there may be as many as hundreds of millions of planets like our earth.

The Bible is not a Book about philosophy or science as we usually think of these subjects, but it reveals the reasons for what are the greatest of all riddles to the scientists: Why were the earth and the human race created?

As an author unfolds his plot at the end of his book, so also does God in the final chapters of Revelation. Here the mystery of God is finished (Rev. 10: 7). Here the divine plan, concealed from the foundation of the world, is unveiled for all who have faith to see.

Through the centuries, part by part, from Old Testament prophets to New Testament apostles, God put His Book together. And it describes the most magnificent plan ever conceived. It should be a fact of intense interest that God took many centuries to write a Book and ended it with wedding scenes—Bridegroom, Bride, Bridal Supper, and Bridal City, which is the New Jerusalem.

In these final disclosures of God's mysteries, it is evident that His plan needed people. It is a people-purpose and it began when God said: "Let us make man in our image, after our likeness. . . . So God created man in his own image, in the image of God created he him." Much of the Bible is about people. If everything about people were removed from the Bible, how much of it would be left?

The peoples of the earth are represented in the Bible by the metaphors of two women. The faithful Church is represented by a bride and the unfaithful church by a harlot. Each woman is described as a "mystery." Paul said the Bride Church is "a great mystery" (Eph. 5:32). And the revealing angel explained to John the mystery of the Harlot Church represented by "the great whore" (Rev. 17:1). All the Bible deals with these two mysteries. The teachings of Jesus and Paul are especially concerned with them.

The true and false churches have appeared side by side in all church history—from Exodus to Revelation. The Bride is symbolic of the true church. Faithful Israel was the Wife of Jehovah-husband by right of the Covenant of Wedlock at Sinai. The harlot is the symbol of the unfaithful church, and the words "harlot," "whoredom," "adultery," "fornication" were used frequently by the true prophets to describe Israel's unfaithfulness to Jehovah. The Harlot Church has always been a *world* church.

Revelation 18:9 says the kings of the earth have committed fornication with this harlot and have "lived deliciously with her." Proud of her world alliances and domination over world rulers, she says: "I sit a queen and am no widow" (v. 7). She is not a widow because she is married to apostate Christendom and to her Antichrist-king whose queen she is. Boastful in her false security, she says she shall "see no sorrow" (v. 7). Her false prophets gave this false security to apostate Israel and false prophets are giving it to apostate Christendom today.

By *World Church* we mean that system of universal religion described in Revelation 17-18. The prophecies do not stress organizational union of these religions, but they do stress the fact that they all "have been made drunk with the wine of her [the harlot's] fornication" (Rev. 17:2). However, a vast organizational union is now being formed. A few years ago I heard a high ranking Roman Catholic dignitary say it was their purpose to bring the religions of the world into one body. There have been significant developments toward this end and more are now in the making.

The harlot church has been the world church of all nations in all times. When John saw the harlot he saw the past and future of all faithless religion.

> The Church, apostatizing, becomes the harlot.... The harlot is every church that has not Christ's mind.... Corrupt, lifeless Christendom is the harlot, whose aim is the pleasure of the flesh, governed by the spirit of nature and the world.

> The carnal, faithless, worldly elements in all churches—Roman, Greek, and Protestant—tend towards one centre, preparing for the last form of the beast, antichrist.

> The faithless church, instead of reproving, connived at the world's self-indulgent luxury, and sanctioned it by her practice.... Men's carnal mind relishes the apostate church, which gives an opiate to conscience and virtual license to lusts.

The worldliness of the church is the most worldly of worldliness. . . . "Harlot" describes the false church's essential character. She retains human shape, as *woman*—does not become a beast—has the form of godliness but denies its power. Her rightful Husband, Jehovah-Christ, and the goods of His house are no longer her all, but she runs after the vain and visible things of the world. The fullest form of whoredom is where the Church wishes to be a worldly power, makes flesh her arm, uses unholy means for holy ends, spreads her dominion by sword or money, fascinates men by sensuous ritualism, (and) becomes "mistress of ceremonies" to the dignitaries of the world.—*Jamieson, Fausset & Brown Commentary*, V. 6, pp. 714-716, Wm. B. Eerdmans Co., Grand Rapids, Mich., 1945.

In Revelation 17:5, John gives a further description of the Harlot Church:

And upon her forehead was a name written, MYSTERY, BABYLON THE GREAT, THE MOTHER OF HARLOTS AND ABOMINATIONS OF THE EARTH.

In ancient times it was customary for harlots to identify themselves by a mark on the forehead. There is a reference to this in Jeremiah 3:1-3, where Jeremiah, dealing with the whoredom of the Jews, said that Judah had "a whore's forehead."

John twice said the harlot is Babylon (5, 18), and that she is the mother of harlots and "abominations" of the earth—meaning all that is loathsome and displeasing to God. As the mother-harlot she procreates in others the same spirit of fornication that is her essential characteristic. She begets a degenerate Church in all nations that have been "made drunk by the wine of her fornication" (17:2). She dazzles the inhabited earth with her power and magnificence and "reigns over the kings of the earth." She fascinates kings and rulers into conformity to her likeness, and universal spiritual abomination is the result.

When John saw the harlot he was struck with amazement at how the Church could degenerate to a world prostitute. The name written on her forehead is *Mystery*. This indicates there is something about her not easily understood. Her true character is concealed, and multitudes united to this harlot system do not know that it will fall into the hands of Antichrist (Rev. 17:3, 7). Great is our need of the Holy Spirit to give us discernment of this satanic mystery.

The harlot is called a "great city." The Bride is also called a "great city" (Rev. 21:10).

> Babylon is: Every nation, city, community, or person who shall become in God's sight what Babylon was. Be like Babylon, and you are Babylon. Her doom is yours, and her final fate yours also.

> The "great city Babylon" . . . is the whole kingdom of evil . . . the wickedness of all kingdoms. . . . In this city you will find not only the evils of the Roman Catholic Church, but of all churches, of all institutions, of all countries and climes.

> Wherever professedly Christian men have thought the world's favor better than its reproach; wherever they have esteemed its honors a more desirable possession than its shame; wherever they have courted ease rather than welcomed suffering, have loved self-indulgence rather than self-sacrifice—there has been a part of the spirit of Babylon.—*The Pulpit Commentary*, V. 51, pp. 420, 439, 440, 446, Funk & Wagnalls Co., New York, undated.

The second coming of Christ is related to sensational prophetic events—especially to the judgment of the Whore-church and the wedding of the Bride-church.

> And after these things I heard a great voice of much people in heaven, saying, Alleluia; Salvation, and glory, and honour, and power, unto the Lord our God:

For true and righteous are his judgments: for he hath judged the great whore, which did corrupt the earth with her fornication, and hath avenged the blood of his servants at her hand.

And again they said, Alleluia. And her smoke rose up forever and ever . . .

And I heard as it were the voice of a great multitude, and as the voice of many waters, and as the voice of mighty thunderings, saying, Alleluia: for the Lord God omnipotent reigneth.

Let us be glad and rejoice, and give honour to him: for the marriage of the Lamb is come, and his wife hath made herself ready.

And to her was granted that she should be arrayed in fine linen, clean and white: for the fine linen is the righteousness of saints.

And he saith unto me, Write, Blessed are they which are called unto the marriage supper of the Lamb. And he saith unto me, These are the true sayings of God.—Rev. 19:1-9

The destructive judgment upon the harlot brings much rejoicing to all heaven. This whorish religious system cannot be redeemed and must be destroyed; her apostasy—like a deadly cancer—cannot be cured. This goddess of lust—this amorous mistress of the nations—and her apostate lovers both receive the full fury of the divine vengeance for their desertion of the Bridegroom.

In contrast, nowhere in all Scripture is there greater rejoicing than for the Lamb's wedding day. A great multitude, with thunderous hosannas, announce: "The marriage of the Lamb is come, and his wife hath made herself ready." This is the event that all heaven is waiting for. It is the fulfillment of the mystery "kept secret from the foundation of the world." (Twenty-five times in Revelation Jesus is "The Lamb.")

The angel seems to have had a particular desire to show John the Lamb's wife:

> And there came unto me one of the seven angels which had the seven vials full of the seven last plagues, and talked with me, saying, Come hither, I will shew thee the bride, the Lamb's wife.
>
> And he carried me away in the spirit to a great and high mountain, and shewed me that great city, the holy Jerusalem, descending out of heaven from God,
>
> Having the glory of God: and her light was like unto a stone most precious, even like a jasper stone, clear as crystal.—Rev. 21:9-11

John said the smoke of the Babylonian harlot's ruin "rose up forever and ever." But, the Bride is united in eternal wedlock to her Bridegroom and becomes His Queen in the bridal-city. And she will reign with Him forever in this capital of the new universe.

From the time that John had been called to be an apostle when he was a young man, he had been given revelations of the divine mysteries. But the magnitude and grandeur of these final disclosures caused him to fall at the feet of the revealing angel.

Our purpose then will be to look into these Bride-Harlot mysteries and see them unveiled. Our study will not be lengthy but it will be sufficient to see what the Bible is all about. We shall see why God took 15 centuries to write a Book and closed it with wedding scenes.

2

Jehovah-Husband and Israel-Wife

The covenant that God made with Israel at Sinai was a Covenant of Wedlock. It was based on the Abrahamic covenant and was a major development toward the ultimate covenant objective as seen at the end of the Book of Revelation. This covenant-plan has moved through various stages through the centuries, and it is having an expansive fulfillment in our time as it progresses toward its consummation.

Covenant-God desired to make further revelations of Himself to the world but needed human channels to accomplish this purpose. There would be new unfoldings of the wedding-plan. He added new promises to the covenant and expanded it to an ever-increasing magnitude. Israel was chosen as His betrothed and He told them the reason for His liberation of them from their Egyptian oppressors:

> Ye have seen what I did unto the Egyptians, and how I bare you on eagles' wings, and brought you unto myself.

> Now therefore, if ye will obey my voice indeed, and keep my covenant, then ye shall be a peculiar treasure unto me above all people: for all the earth is mine:

> And ye shall be unto me a kingdom of priests, and an holy nation.—Ex. 19:4-6

God often reminded Israel of this covenant at Sinai. We now look at a few references to show that it was a Covenant of Betrothal, and we shall also see how the subject is interwoven in the Scriptures.

In Isaiah 49:18, the true Church shall be clothed and adorned "as a bride doeth." In 54:5, Zion is compared to a bride: "For thy Maker is thine husband; the Lord of hosts is his name." As "Maker" of the covenant and the bridal kingdom, this Name is His assurance that He will be the Husband of all true Israelites.

> I will greatly rejoice in the Lord, my soul shall be joyful in my God, for he hath clothed me with the garments of salvation, he hath covered me with the robe of righteousness, as a bridegroom decketh himself with ornaments, and as a bride adorneth herself with her jewels.—Isa. 61:10

In 62:4, Isaiah said that Israel would be called "Hephzibah, and thy land Beulah: for the Lord delighteth in thee, and thy land shall be married." "Hephzibah" means: "My delight is in her," and "Beulah" means "married."

> For as a young man marrieth a virgin, so shall thy sons marry thee: and as the bridegroom rejoiceth over the bride, so shall thy God rejoice over thee (as a bridegroom thrills to his bride, so shall your God thrill to you—Moffatt).—Isa. 62:5

The prophets often used this bridegroom-bride relationship, and the true Church was given the assurance that they would not be deserted as a forsaken woman but received forever into the bridal kingdom.

Jeremiah also tells about the nuptial-bond. Various translations give different renderings of the following verses but we take them from the King James Version.

After Israel had jilted her divine Lover, He opened His arms in forgiving love and invited her to return: "Turn, O backsliding children, saith the Lord; for

I am married unto you" (3:14). And in 31:32, God said He was "an husband" unto Israel.

Ezekiel adds details to the picture which throws light on the ancient Jewish betrothal. He describes the espousal garments, ornaments, and the beauty given to the bride by the Bridegroom. All this was more than metaphor—it was spiritual reality. God continually reminded Israel about the Betrothal at Sinai:

> I clothed thee also with broidered work, and shod thee with badgers' skin, and I girded thee about with fine linen, and I covered thee with silk.
>
> I decked thee also with ornaments, and I put bracelets upon thy hands, and a chain on thy neck.
>
> And I put a jewel on thy forehead, and earrings in thine ears, and a beautiful crown upon thine head.
>
> Thus wast thou decked with gold and silver; and thy raiment was of fine linen, and silk, and broidered work: thou didst eat fine flour, and honey and oil: and thou wast exceeding beautiful, and thou didst prosper into a kingdom.
>
> And thy renown went forth among the heathen for thy beauty: for it was perfect through my comeliness, which I had put upon thee, saith the Lord God.
>
> But thou didst trust in thine own beauty, and playedst the harlot because of thy renown, and pouredst out thy fornications on every one that passed by . . .
> —Ezek. 16:10-15

In verse 8, God spoke of the spreading of a skirt over the betrothed, which was another custom of the ancient espousal. And in many parts of the East this practice has continued to our time. It indicated a proposal of marriage and that the man accepted the woman into his protection and care.

> Now when I passed by thee, and looked upon thee, behold, thy time was the time of love; and I spread

my skirt over thee, and covered thy nakedness:
yea, I sware unto thee, and entered into a covenant
with thee, saith the Lord God, and thou becamest
mine.—Ezek. 16:8

Skirt is the part of a garment below the waist.
Ruth says to Boaz, Cast thy skirt over me, Ruth
3:9, that is, Take me into thy protection by taking
me to be thy wife. It is spoken in allusion to the
ancient custom or ceremony of the bridegroom's
spreading the skirt of his garment over the bride;
to signify his right to her, his authority over her,
and his obligation to protect her.

So also in Ezekiel 16:8. I spread my skirt over thee:
I betrothed thee, and engaged by covenant to love,
cherish, protect, and guard thee.—*Cruden's Una-
bridged Concordance,* Alexander Cruden, p. 450,
Baker Book House, Grand Rapids, Mich., 1959.

In passing briefly through the prophets for a
sketch of our subject, we come to Hosea who helps
to fill in the outline.

The forsaken Lover complained that His adulterous Wife had "transgressed my covenant" (8:1) by
forbidden alliances with heathen nations, and had defiled herself with passionate embraces of their gods.
"Israel is defiled . . . for the *spirit* of whoredoms is
in the midst of them" (5:3-4).

The Mother had borne "children of whoredoms"
(1:2; 2:4), but the Husband foresaw that a future
Israel would love Him and that the prophetic promises could be fulfilled in them. Three times He spoke
of the eternal marriage when the true Israel will
call Him "Ishi," that is, "My Husband" (2:16-20).

And I will betroth thee unto me for ever; yea, I
will betroth thee unto me in righteousness, and in
judgment, and in lovingkindness, and in mercies.

I will even betroth thee unto me in *faithfulness:*
and thou shalt know the Lord.—Hosea 2:19, 20

We shall see next how this wedding story passes into the New Testament and how it all connects with Christ's coming and the World Church.

> The bride is the familiar Old Testament figure expressive of the people in their close relation to God (Isa. 54:5; Hosea 2:18; Ps. 45). This figure passes into the New Testament.—*The Expositors Greek Testament,* V. 1, p. 720, Wm. B. Eerdmans Pub. Co., Grand Rapids, Mich., 1956.

> ... the Covenant-union between God and Israel was not only compared to marriage, but the Tabernacle and Temple designated as "the bridal chambers."—*The Life and Times of Jesus the Messiah,* Edersheim, Alfred, V. 1, pp. 663-664, Wm. B. Eerdmans Pub. Co., Grand Rapids, Mich. Thirty-Sixth Printing.

3

The Jewish Betrothal and Christ's Coming

This marriage of Christ and His Church is further unveiled in the New Testament. It is a marvel of revelation in the Scriptures, and it is the summation of Biblical revelation. All unfulfilled prophecy is related to it. It is "a spectacle . . . to angels," and they gaze intently at the earth as the Bride-church is being formed and prepared for the wedding (I Cor. 4:9; I Pet. 1:12).

The ministry of John the Baptist was "to make ready a people prepared for the Lord" (Luke 1:17). Jesus said that John was "more than a prophet," and that "among them born of women there hath not risen a greater than John the Baptist." Moses and Elijah, with all their miracles, were not greater than John who "did no miracle." Why then was John *more* than a prophet? What was the reason for this unique honor and high rank among the prophets?

John, in preparing the way for Christ, said that he was "the friend of the bridegroom." This expression was familiar to Jewish ears. When John had finished his work as the Bridegroom's friend, he said: "This my joy therefore is fulfilled." He put it like this:

> He that hath the bride is the bridegroom: but the friend of the bridegroom, which standeth and heareth him, rejoiceth greatly because of the bride-

groom's voice: this my joy therefore is fulfilled.
—John 3:29

On the meaning of "friend" of the bridegroom, leading sources say:

> John is only like the *paranymphios* or "the friend of the bridegroom." His office is to bring bridegroom and bride together.—*Word Studies in the New Testament,* Robertson, A. T., V. 5, p. 56, Broadman Press, Nashville, Tenn. 1932.

> (John) was to see that his delicate task was crowned with success; and of this he was assured when he stood and heard the bridegroom directly welcoming his bride ("voice of the bridegroom" as symbol of joy, Jer. 7:34; 16:9).

> This is the joy which John claims for himself, and the joy of the bridegroom's friend, who arranged the marriage, and this joy is attained in Christ's welcoming to Himself the people whom John has prepared for Him and directed to Him.—*The Expositors Greek Testament,* V. 1, p. 720, Wm. B. Eerdmans Publishing Co., Grand Rapids, Mich., 1956.

> The term [friend] is appropriate to Judea, the groomsmen not being customary in Galilee. In Judea there were two groomsmen, one for the bridegroom, the other for the bride. Before marriage, they acted as intermediaries between the couple; at the wedding they offered gifts, waited upon the bride and bridegroom, and attended them to the bridal chamber. It was the duty of the friend of the bridegroom to present him to the bride, and after the marriage to maintain proper terms between the parties, and especially to defend the bride's good name.

> The Rabbinical writings speak of Moses as the friend of the bridegroom who leads out the bride to meet Jehovah at Sinai (Ex. 19:17): and describe Michael and Gabriel as acting as the friends of the bridegroom to our first parents when the Almighty himself took the cup of blessing and spoke the benediction. The Baptist represents himself as standing in the same relation to Jesus.—*Word Studies in*

the New Testament, Vincent, M. R., V. 2, p. 105, Wm. B. Eerdmans Publishing Co., Grand Rapids, Mich., 1957.

Dr. Alfred Edersheim, the international New Testament Jewish authority, wrote the following about the betrothal of Joseph and Mary (Matt. 1: 18).

> From that moment, Mary was the betrothal wife of Joseph; their relationship was as sacred as if they had already been wedded. Any breach of it would be treated as adultery; nor could the bond be dissolved except, as after marriage, by regular divorce.
> —*The Life and Times of Jesus the Messiah,* V. 1, p. 150, Wm. B. Eerdmans Publishing Co., Grand Rapids, Mich., 1953.

An interesting example of a betrothal arranged by a friend of the bridegroom is in the 24th chapter of Genesis when Abraham sent his servant to get a bride for his son Isaac. This story illustrates the ancient betrothal ceremony, and the bringing of bride and bridegroom together by a friend (*paranymphios*). Among Oriental tribes, the most important part of the marriage was the espousal ceremony. In Genesis 24, the entire chapter, except one verse, gives details about the betrothal of Isaac and Rebekkah, and the one verse tells about Isaac taking Rebekkah to be his wife. The friend had accomplished his mission when he brought Rebekkah to Isaac.

At the ceremony, gifts were bestowed upon the bride for accepting the marriage proposal. Isaac's groomsman gave Rebekkah gifts of "jewels of gold, silver, and *raiment.*" He also gave gifts to Rebekkah's family.

The betrothal ceremony among Jews varied in different countries and times, but the sanctity of the covenant was universally accepted by Jews. Violation of the covenant in early times was a deadly offense in the family life of the nation, and divine justice looked upon it with the severest degree of condemnation. To profane Jehovah's law of wedlock was a "sin unto death." It was classed with murder and put in the category of capital crimes. Even after the death penalty was abolished, a Jew had to divorce a guilty partner with compulsory dissolution.

God reminded Israel of the death penalty by stoning and burning for infidelity (Gen. 38:24; Lev. 21:9; Deut. 22:22), and warned them that because of "thy whoredoms with thy lovers," He would deal with them as with "women that break wedlock . . . and I will give thee blood in fury and *jealousy*" (Ezek. 16:36-38). The horrible history of Israel's captivities and slaughter—even to modern times—is impressive evidence that He did.

In the New Testament, the Bridegroom also warned the churches of a spiritual death penalty because of their infidelity expressed in the word "fornication" (Rev. 2:12-24):

> And I will kill her children with death; and all the churches shall know that I am he which searcheth the reins and hearts; and I will give unto every one of you according to your works.—Rev. 2:23

The only hope held out to them was repentance. His ultimatum was:

> Repent; or else I will come unto thee quickly, and will fight against thee with the sword of my mouth. —Rev. 2:16

What an awful statement from the loving Christ! He will fight against a church with a sword! God often threatened harlot-Israel with the "sword" of His vengeance. The worse stroke of the divine sword has yet to come. Jesus spoke about it when He told of the coming judgments upon a harlot world: "For these be the days of vengeance . . ." (Luke 21:22).

Why is it that many ministers who preach so much about the love of God never get around to these truths about His jealous vengeance upon those who persistently reject that love?

Great is the need among the churches to repent of their loving the world, money, and pleasure. And because they have not repented, the threatened death sentence has fallen upon them and they lie barren in spiritual death. They have yielded to the harlot's advances for ease and popularity. The "offence of the cross" has ceased. The "reproach of Christ" is gone.

The old penalty of death by burning will be inflicted upon the World-harlot. God said He will gather her lovers against her and they will "burn her with fire" (Rev. 17:16). All who are joined to the Harlot will perish with her. Paul wrote: "Shall I then take the members of Christ, and make them the members of an harlot? God forbid. What? know ye not that he which is joined to an harlot is one body?" (I Cor. 6:15-16).

Israel violated her covenant with Jehovah when she entered into alliances with unbelieving nations, and was defiled when she bowed to their gods. The prophets often rebuked them because they "transgressed the covenant." To love Jehovah by being a separate and holy people was the first law of the covenant, and this is also required in the terms of the New Covenant:

> Be ye not unequally yoked together with unbelievers: for what fellowship hath righteousness with unrighteousness? and what communion hath light with darkness?
>
> And what agreement hath the temple of God with idols? for ye are the temple of the living God. . . .

> Wherefore come out from among them, and be ye
> separate, saith the Lord, and touch not the unclean
> thing; and I will receive you.—II Cor. 6:14, 16, 17

This *separation* was the heart of the Jewish nuptial vows. The marriage ceremony was called *kiddushin*, a rabbinical expression derived from the Hebrew *qadesh*, meaning "consecrated" or "sanctified." It was a ceremony of sanctification—the two parties consecrated to each other for a holy purpose. The most important vow was: "I become sanctified unto thee, according to the law of Moses and Israel."

Throughout the New Testament, the word "sanctify" or some cognate word is related to this wedding scene.

There were seven benedictions at the ceremony, and the first was a blessing of sanctification. After taking the vow and receiving the blessing of sanctification, the bride was considered a queen.

It was a tradition not only for the bride to wear a white gown but also for the bridegroom to be clothed in a white robe. There seems to be an allusion to this in Revelation 3:4, where the Bridegroom promised the faithful in Sardis:

> Thou hast a few names even in Sardis which have
> not *defiled* their garments; and they shall walk with
> me in white: for they are worthy.

But to the worldly and self-satisfied church at Laodicea, which had been corrupted with the "spirit of whoredom," He sent this message:

> I counsel thee to buy of me gold tried in the fire,
> that thou mayest be rich; and white raiment, that
> thou mayest be clothed, and that the shame of thy
> nakedness do not appear.—Rev. 3:18

It is also significant that the multitude of the redeemed that John saw in heaven was "clothed with white robes," and the Bride was "arrayed in fine linen, clean and white," and those who return with the Bridegroom when He comes to destroy the Harlot are clothed in white (Rev. 7:9, 13; 19:8, 14).

The Jewish marital covenant was conditional and could be dissolved for unfaithfulness. When repeated attempts for a reconciliation had failed, Jehovah gave faithless Israel a "bill of divorce" and put her away. This is referred to in the New Testament when God said that Israel "continued not in my covenant, and I regarded them not [abandoned them]" (Jer. 3:8; Heb. 8:9).

In later times, the practice of breaking a glass was added to the ceremony. Various explanations are given for this, one being that it was a warning to the couple that as a blow shattered the glass, so also unchastity could shatter the home. If anyone knew that the betrothed parties had been unfaithful to the covenant and withheld the information, the penalty was excommunication. The covenant oath required that both parties forsake all other lovers. It was a vow of virginity. "Virgin" means *separated*.

Washing and anointing were part of the preparation for the wedding (Ruth 3:3; Esther 2:12). This reminds us of Ephesians 5:25-27:

> Christ also loved the church, and gave himself for it;
>
> That he might sanctify and cleanse it with the washing of water by the word,
>
> That he might present it to himself a glorious church, not having spot, or wrinkle, or any such thing; but that it should be holy and without blemish.

This picture of purity stands in contrast to the "filthiness" of the harlot's fornication (Rev. 17:4).

This filthiness means "all that is contrary to purity" (Vine).

There was much excitement in preparation for the wedding, and various festivities and merrymaking were connected with it. There was also much feasting. The ancient wedding feast lasted seven days and was accompanied by continuous musical performances (Judges 14:12). When Jesus was asked why His disciples did not fast, as did the disciples of John, He explained:

> Can the children of the bridechamber mourn, as long as the bridegroom is with them? but the days will come, when the bridegroom shall be taken from them, and then shall they fast.—Matt. 9:15

When John, in prophetic vision, saw the Bride of Christ, and the revealing angel said: "Blessed are they which are called unto the marriage supper of the Lamb," he was so overcome by the grandeur and glory of it all that he fell at the feet of the angel (Rev. 19:9-10).

There are other details of the ancient Jewish wedding, especially in *The Song of Solomon,* but these are sufficient to show the background of our subject. Details not found in the Scriptures can be verified from various Jewish sources, including Jewish encyclopedias and *The Jewish Marriage Anthology* (Philip and Hanna Goodman, Jewish Publication Society, Philadelphia, Pa., 1965).

When John the Baptist left the wilderness and began his ministry, he won the heart of the nation, and "all men mused in their hearts whether he were the Christ, or not." But when John denied that he was the Christ and directed the people to Jesus as the Messiah, he fell into disfavor. The nation's leaders rejected his message . . . that Jesus was

Israel's Bridegroom. The groomsman was beheaded and they crucified the Bridegroom on Skull Hill outside Harlot City (Isa. 1:21).

4

The Called Church

Our word "church" comes from the Greek word *ekklesia,* and before it was used in the New Testament it had the meaning of "calling out and assembling together for a definite purpose." It was used among Greeks of a body of citizens who were summoned together to discuss or transact business of the state. In the Septuagint it was used of a gathering of Israelites who were called together for a special purpose. One of the most frequently quoted Scriptures is Romans 8:28, but it is one that most Christians seem to have a vague understanding of. Let's look at it again with part of its context.

> And we know that all things work together for good to them that *love* God, to them who are the called according to his purpose.
>
> For whom he did foreknow, he also did predestinate to be conformed to the image of his Son, that he might be the firstborn among many brethren.
>
> Moreover whom he did predestinate, them he also called: and whom he called, them he also justified: and whom he justified, them he also glorified.
>
> What shall we say then to these things? If God be for us, who can be against us?

God's church-plan is a people-plan, and God mysteriously works all things together for good to those who are called to this purpose which will consummate in the events described in the last chapters of Revelation. A strong faith is necessary to believe, accept, and live this truth. It will be at the sounding of the seventh angel (Rev. 10:7) that "the mystery of God" is finished. The word *mystery* indicates there is something about it that is yet unknown.

The above texts present what was a fundamental concept with Paul. God, being all-wise and knowing all things "from the foundation of the world," foresaw those who would love Him, and because of their love for Him, they would be "conformed to the image of his Son." They were then predestinated or forechosen and called to His eternal purpose; and as God is *for* us, nothing can be against us so as to defeat this purpose.

Predestination becomes distorted and hopelessly confused when it is detached from "love," "justified," and "conformed to the image of his Son." Those who bear His moral image now shall also bear His heavenly likeness. Apart from this Christlikeness, the word "purpose" has no meaning. Nor does the word "predestinate" have any meaning.

Our Lord said, "I will build my church; and the gates of hell shall not prevail against it." Christ is building His church with those who are called to His Bride-purpose. Their love, faith, and yearning for His likeness mean much to Him and He loves and cherishes them. They are an invincible spiritual fortress because they are supercharged by the power of His Spirit, and "they shall never perish."

The Bride Church was something new out of the divine mysteries. The inhabitants of all the created universe had never seen the like of this before. And this people-purpose began its New Testament formation with a call to repentance. John was the groomsman of the Bridegroom, and "in those days came John the Baptist, preaching in the wilderness of Judaea, and saying, Repent ye: for the kingdom of heaven is at hand." He was "the voice," calling the Bride to the Bridegroom.

The penitent accepted the call and came in repentance to be baptized. But the leaders of the adulterous nation—"the Pharisees and lawyers rejected the counsel of God against themselves, being not baptized of him." To be baptized of John, they had to confess they were sinners, because it was a "baptism unto repentance," and they refused a baptism that was for sinners and Gentile proselytes. They were born the covenant sons of Abraham and did not need the baptism of the strange prophet from the wilderness.

They also rejected the testimony of The Voice about Christ because the humble prophet from Nazareth did not fit into their grandiose visions of an earthly Messianic empire.

John's message to that apostate nation was like the flashing of a two-edged sword that he thrust deep into their adulterous consciences. He turned against the unrepentant with a fierce rebuke, and warned them that God's ax of judgment was laid at the root of the tree, ready to cut it down. There must be a moral reformation to avert the threatened doom. He was specific about their sins and urged them to "flee from the wrath to come."

If John had only preached about sin in a general manner, he could have saved his head. But he was specific about it to all classes, and soon the executioner's sword slashed the throat of The Voice. There had always been attempts to silence the voices of the prophets—and there always will be.

John was the keynoter for New Testament preachers. His mission was not a failure because he began the call to gather the Bride. His message of repentance, righteousness, and judgment to come, must also be our message as we herald the coming of the Bridegroom. The call that preceded Christ's first coming must also be the call for His second coming.

The Bridegroom continued the call begun by His groomsman. When John heard "the voice of the Bridegroom," he said he rejoiced greatly, and, "this my joy therefore is fulfilled." The Bridegroom's voice is a joy to the Bride, but not to those who, having ears to hear, hear not.

When Jesus told about His sheep, He said, "My sheep hear my voice, and I know them, and they follow me." When He calls His sheep they recognize Him, and follow Him. They also recognize the voices of strangers and will not follow them.

When Jesus was on trial before Pilate, He talked about His kingdom and the subjects of His kingdom: "To this end was I born, and for this cause came I into the world, that I should bear witness unto the truth. Everyone that is of the truth heareth my voice." Pilate appears to have been impatient and skeptical at this. What kind of king is this? What is this truth?

A kingdom of truth! Only this King has such a dominion, and every subject of this kingdom loves and obeys this truth. And like their King, it was for this kingdom that they were born, and for this cause that they came into the world. To all who love Him and hear His voice, He is "the Way, and the Truth, and the Life." In I Thessalonians 2:12, Paul said that God "hath called you unto his kingdom."

This Called-church was an essential part of apostolic teaching. Let's look at a few of the references.

Paul told the Romans they were "the called of Jesus Christ" and that they were the "beloved of God, called to be saints" (Rom. 1:6-7). They were called to be the choice possession of Jesus Christ —"the heritage of the Lord." They were first called to repentance; then they were called to be His sanctified ones. This part of the calling is as necessary as the first part. Why repent if they did not qualify to be "called to the marriage supper of the Lamb"? It seems strange that many professing Christians have no interest in this part of God's call that requires them to be saints. Paul also told the Corinthians they were called to be saints, and that they were "called unto the fellowship of his Son Jesus Christ our Lord" (I Cor. 1:2, 9).

Paul was pressing toward the heavenly calling when he wrote: "I press toward the mark for the prize of the high calling of God in Christ Jesus" (Phil. 3:14). Like a runner exerting himself to get to the goal, Paul was leaving earthly things behind and pushing upward. He was always trying to get higher because that's where the prize was. This Bride-purpose is a high calling. It originates and ends in heaven, and all the Bride are "partakers of the heavenly calling" (Heb. 3:1). The low moral state of many professing Christians is inconsistent with this calling to heaven.

Paul repeated the same truth to the Thessalonians: "For God hath not called us unto uncleanness, but unto holiness." And in II Timothy 1:9, he said that God "hath saved us, and called us with an holy calling." We must "walk worthy of the calling wherewith ye are called" (Eph. 4:1).

The Holy Spirit continued to stress the importance of this truth through the apostle Peter:

> But as he which hath called you is holy, so be ye
> holy in all manner of conversation.

> Because it is written: Be ye holy; for I am holy.

Christ requires His followers to be what He is.
"As he is, so are we in this world." The Bride must
take on the moral character of the Bridegroom. "By
what He requires of me, I know what God Himself
must be."

Peter, like John the Baptist, warned the people
about the delusion of a false security. If they had
faith for salvation, there would be external evidence
of it. He told them to "make your calling and election sure: for if ye do these things, ye shall never
fall" (II Pet. 1:5-10). Peter taught here that salvation is sure for those who "make" it sure. They
were called to practice diligence, moral character,
temperance, godliness, faith, kindness and love. If
they would *do* these things, they would make their
salvation certain because God had made these things
necessary in His calling and election of them. It is
a deception to separate love, faith, and godliness
from calling and election.

When Christ returns to set up His kingdom, the
Babylon-Harlot and all the powers of Satan will oppose Him. Revelation 17:14 describes it:

> These shall make war with the Lamb, and the Lamb
> shall overcome them: for he is Lord of lords, and
> King of kings: and they that are with him are
> called, and chosen, and faithful.

This text shows how the calling, choice, and
faithfulness of those with Christ is related to their
sharing His victory over Antichrist and the powers
of his world empire. To this final victory they have
been called; to this they have been chosen; and to
this they have been faithful. It is the desire of Christ

that His faithful ones will share this triumph with Him.

Christ, on earth, was the gentle and loving Lamb. At Calvary, He took on all the powers of hell and defeated them as the Lamb. But when He comes at the battle of Armageddon He will be a different Lamb. His enemies will run into the mountains and dens to hide from "the wrath of the Lamb." Did anyone ever see an angry Lamb? Will it not be worth everything to be faithful now that we may be with Him and share in His greatest victory?

The called-chosen-faithful ones will also sit down at the marriage supper: "Blessed are they which are called to the marriage supper of the Lamb." To this we are also called. The angel did not describe this event but simply said those are blessed who are called to it. The glory and grandeur of it cannot be imagined.

God's call to the kingdom is sounding out to all the earth today, and the faithful ones are coming out to a life of obedience and separation. This kingdom is for all—"as many as the Lord our God shall call." And these called ones have the same obedient faith of Abraham, "the father of us all": "By faith Abraham, when he was called to go out . . . went out" to a life of separation and consecration to God's purpose (Heb. 11:8).

This calling out of the world and the harlot system will continue until the end of the age, as we see in Revelation 18:4, immediately before the destruction of Harlot-Babylon:

> And I heard another voice from heaven, saying, Come out of her, my people, that ye be not partakers of her sins, and that ye receive not of her plagues.

Paul said that God, in the secrecy of His working, is making all things work together for good to them that love Him. Some quote this promise who do not have the right to it because they do not love God. It will only work for those who love Him and have faith to accept it.

True believers do not stumble at the mystery of this. They know that the new birth is a mystery, and that the resurrection will be a mystery, and everything between the two is a mystery. We cannot comprehend it but "we know" it is true. The finite cannot understand the Infinite, but it can love and obey.

To bring our Scriptures together and sum up, we conclude that God's calling is for the purpose of forming a *Church*—a body of people, called to repentance, to love Him, to be justified and glorified, to be holy, to be saints, and to be conformed to the image of Christ.

It is a heavenly calling, a holy calling, a high calling to God's eternal prize, a calling to share His victory at Armageddon, a calling to the marriage supper, a call to holiness and to the Kingdom.

If you want to know what is of God, and what is not, put it to this test: Does it obey God's call to holiness?

"Faithful is he that calleth you, who also will do it," which means that God will complete the work of this calling (I Thess. 5:24).

5

The Tested Church

We have seen that God calls people together for a purpose; then He calls them out to separation and testing. He proves that He may approve, and what is approved is "chosen." The remnants are the proved-approved-chosen people. There has been much dispute among theologians whether God's covenants with men are conditional or unconditional. But, if they are unconditional, what is the reason for the provings?

God led Israel into the wilderness crises, "and there he proved them" (Ex. 15:25). God said He would "prove them, whether they will walk in my way, or no" (Ex. 16:4). God later referred to a test which proved that they did not love Him: "I proved thee at the waters of Meribah [Strife]" (Ps. 81:7). "For thou, O God, hast proved us: thou hast tried us, as silver is tried" (Ps. 66:10). These and other similar texts show that God's dealings with Israel were conditional, Moses told them in his farewell message:

> And thou shalt remember all the way which the
> Lord thy God led thee these forty years in the wil-
> derness, to humble thee, and to prove thee, to know
> what was in thine heart, whether thou wouldest keep
> his commandments, or no.—Deut. 8:2

In Biblical use, as in Classical Greek, the words "examine, try, test, prove" contain the technical idea of putting something to a test to determine if it is genuine or counterfeit. That which endures the test is genuine, and that which fails the test is counterfeit. In some cases, where men are spoken of as having been *tried,* it does not mean merely that they have been tested but that they have victoriously passed the test and continue to do so.

The testing of metals and money to illustrate God's provings of people is one of the most important truths in the Bible, and it is essentially related to Christ's coming and the World Church. These provings do not reveal anything to God because He knows all things, from beginning to ending, but they are necessary that men may know their own hearts. After revealing Israel's true character to them, God said: "Israel is to me become dross: all they are brass, and tin, and iron, and lead, in the midst of the furnace; they are even the dross of silver" (Ezek. 22:18).

There are other kinds of testing in the Bible, as the removal of impurities from gold and silver. The refiner knows that the ore he throws into the refining pot is not all gold nor all dross. He knows that the fire will separate one from the other and the pure metal will come forth. This is what Job meant when he said, "When he hath tried me, I shall come forth as gold" (23:10), and Job did have some dross to be burnt out of his life.

The test that we are primarily concerned with is that which determines what is genuine and what is counterfeit—what is approved and what is disapproved—what is true and what is false Christianity. We shall look at a few of the many references in the New Testament to show the continuity of this truth in the Scriptures. There are some excellent examples of Jesus testing men but we'll start with Paul in Acts 20:29-30.

Even the work of an apostle had to be cleansed

of defilement and Paul here warned the Ephesian elders that God would purge the church at Ephesus. This was a church of central importance in Paul's labors.

Paul's warning was that "grievous wolves" would enter the church, "not sparing the flock. Also of *your own selves* shall men arise, speaking perverse things, to draw away disciples after them." The purgings came to Ephesus, as they come to churches everywhere. A long and interesting history could be written about this.

Romans 5:3-4. Paul here taught that "tribulation worketh patience; and patience, experience [Gr. *proof*] and proof brings hope." This text says that endurance in Christ produces proof that one has stood the test, and this proof of spiritual character is the ground of hope. Some spiritual experiences come to us by instantaneous workings of the Holy Spirit, but other experiences may require considerable time.

I Corinthians 11:19. "For there must be also heresies among you, that they which are approved may be made manifest among you."

Paul said there "must be" divisions among the Corinthians. They sometimes are necessary and are ordered by God that the approved may be made *manifest* and clearly seen. The genuine are tested for the purpose of being attested. The false-hearted are exposed and recognized as rejected. In divisions, the false choose the wrong but the true choose the right, and God makes this distinction that both may be revealed to men. The choice they make in the trial shows what they are.

Paul's searchings of his converts were exact and rigid. His reason for these examinations was to "know the proof of you, whether ye be obedient in all things." And again, "to prove the sincerity of your love." Paul did not exempt himself from this divine scrutiny, and imposed an austere discipline upon his mind and body, lest, "I myself should be a castaway"—rejected for the prize after running the race. "Castaway" means *rejected,* and the prize is the "crown of life."

In this context, Paul used the illustration of the Olympic athlete who was examined by the judges after the race to see if, by any violation of the rules, he had disqualified himself for the prize. In recent Olympic games, both in Europe and America, athletes were disqualified for the prizes after winning the contests because they broke the rules. Paul, an exact teacher, used a *conditional* contest to illustrate the winning of God's prize for running the Christian race (I Cor. 9:24-27).

Paul would not let them take salvation for granted. Coming to the end of his Corinthian epistles, he was repetitious, and wrote:

> Examine yourselves, whether ye be in the faith; prove your own selves. Know ye not your own selves, how that Jesus Christ is in you, except ye be reprobates?—II Cor. 13:5

The Greek word for "reprobate" (*adokimos*) has critical and decisive meaning in the New Testament. Standard Greek authorities support the following.

> Reprobate (adokimos), signifying 'not standing the test,' rejected ... applied to metals ... Titus 1:16, of the defiled, who are "unto every good work reprobate," i.e., if they are put to the test in regard to any good work (in contrast to their profession) they can only be rejected.—*Expository Dictionary of New Testament Words,* Vine, W. E., V. 3, p. 283, Oliphants Ltd., London, 1948.

> Reprobate means tried and found to be worthless. "Reprobate silver shall men call them, because the

Lord hath rejected them" (Jer. 6:30).—*Pulpit Commentary,* V. 45, p. 313, New York: Funk & Wagnalls Co., undated.

Reprobates, literally, 'not abiding the proof,' worthless—in this case, 2 Cor. 13:5, mere pretended Christians.—*The New Testament for English Readers,* Henry Alford, p. 1157, Chicago: Moody Press, undated.

Paul challenged (the Corinthians) to try themselves, to test themselves, whether they were "in the faith" ... Such tests can be made, unless, alas, they are "Reprobate," the very adjective that Paul held up before himself as a dreadful outcome to be avoided (I Cor. 9:27).—*Word Pictures in the New Testament,* Robertson, A. T., V. 4, p. 270, Broadman Press, Nashville, Tenn., Seventh Printing.

It was basic with Paul that his associates had to be tested for character and faithfulness. They must *"first* be proved" (I Tim. 3:10). Writing to the Philippians about Timothy, Paul said, "Ye know the proof of him"; but John Mark was rejected because he had failed to prove himself, although he was later accepted by Paul after he had won approval.

Paul and Peter wrote about "unfeigned love," and John wrote: "Let us not love in word, but in deed and in truth" (I John 3:18). We have seen much feigned love among professing Christians, and it reminds us of Jesus' denunciation of the hypocrites: "This people draweth nigh unto me with their mouth, and honor me with their lips. but their heart is far from me." The difference between unfeigned and feigned love is the difference between true and false Christians. The former demonstrate their love with *deeds* of love; the latter do not. Paul described them in Titus 1:16: "They profess that they know God; but in works they deny him, being abominable, and disobedient, and unto every good work reprobate."

Paul, always testing and proving, admonished others to do likewise, and in a sweeping order to the Thessalonians, wrote: "Prove all things," and to hold fast to those things that endured the proving. Paul had deep concern for the final result of his work, and three times wrote about his caution that it would not be "in vain." With repeated emphasis on this subject to the Corinthians, Paul made another startling disclosure about the final-day test when all who enter the eternal kingdom must first receive the Refiner's approval:

> For other foundation can no man lay than that is laid, which is Jesus Christ.
>
> Now if any man build upon this foundation gold, silver, precious stones, wood, hay, stubble;
>
> Every man's work, shall be made manifest: for the day shall declare it, because it shall be revealed by fire; and the fire shall try every man's work, of what sort it is.
>
> If any man's work abide which he hath built thereupon, he shall receive a reward.
>
> If any man's work shall be burned, he shall suffer loss: but he himself shall be saved; yet so as by fire.
>
> Know ye not that ye are the temple of God, and that the Spirit of God dwelleth in you?
>
> If any man defile the temple of God, him shall God destroy; for the temple of God is holy, which temple ye are.—I Cor. 3:11-17

Many who have been deceived into believing that they are genuine, must appear before Him who has "eyes like unto a flame of fire," and who "searcheth the reins and hearts." This fiery examination will be so exact that the smallest details of our lives will not escape the searching of His flaming eyes. What an awesome and consuming revelation it will be for many ministers, Christians, and denominational leaders! Paul had a warning for all of us: "Let every man prove his own work..." (Gal. 6:4).

The final test will be an evaluation of each man and his work, methods and motives. If his work passes God's high standards, he shall receive a reward; if not, he shall suffer loss. Many will discover too late that with their cheap methods they built temples of straw. If they had obeyed Paul's admonition to prove their work, they could have produced a work of golden character. To enter the eternal kingdom, one must possess the qualities of that kingdom. "The temple of God is *holy*."

When Malachi saw this judgment-seat of Christ, he was awestruck, and wrote:

> But who may abide the day of his coming? and who shall stand when he appeareth? for he is like a refiner's fire, and like fullers' soap:
>
> And he shall sit as a refiner and purifier of silver: and he shall purify the sons of Levi, and purge them as gold and silver, that they may offer unto the Lord an offering in righteousness.—3:2-3

We go now to Hebrews 11:17, and see how the Holy Spirit continued to repeat this truth in the New Testament: "By faith Abraham, when he was tried, offered up Isaac...."

This, the most severe test in Abraham's life, was not an isolated event—it was not detached from his whole life of faith which began when he was called out of his country to go into a place, "not knowing whither he went." The testing of Abraham was continually in progress. Each event in his life was a link in the whole connection, and it was only "after he had patiently endured, he obtained the promise" (Heb. 6:15). He did not receive, nor to this day has

he received the entire fulfillment of that promise.
For the ultimate accomplishment of that promise
all he yet has is God's covenant word.

Abraham's faith was more than a mental persuasion that God's word was true. It was an obedient
faith that responded to God's commands with what
Jesus said were "the works of Abraham." He was
not justified by the works but by the faith that gen-
erated the works. His outward acts or works were
manifestations of his inward faith. When God saw
that Abraham, under trial, had a living faith that
gave birth to acts of righteousness, "it was accounted
to him [put to his account] for righteousness" (Gal.
3:6).

Abraham did not boast in his works. When put
to trial, and proving his faith, he was "giving glory
to God" (Rom. 4:20). If he had been boastful of his
works, he would have been rejected as disapproved.

Genuine faith glorifies God for His grace that
makes justification possible. Without this grace, faith
and its works would be nothing. Counterfeit faith
produces self-righteousness and glorifies the creature
more than the Creator. It is boastful and vain-glori-
ous, and its self-righteous works are rejected by God
as "filthy rags."

It was on this point of Abraham's faith-works
that Jesus angered the self-righteous Pharisees who
were leaders of the Harlot Church at that time. They
claimed the right to the eternal kingdom of God on
the ground that they were the covenant sons of Abraham. But Jesus said if they were true spiritual sons
of Abraham, they would "do the works of Abraham."
They were doing the "deeds" of their father the
devil. Instead of the evidence of faith, they showed
evidence of unbelief. Instead of proving themselves

sons of God, they proved they were sons of the devil (John 8:33-44).

John the Baptist had previously told them, "Bring forth therefore fruits worthy of repentance." Various translations give the true meaning of this, which is: *Bring forth fruits to prove that you have repented.* This they had failed to do and they were exposed as counterfeits. And their teaching of being forever secure in the Abrahamic covenant was a fraud because they did not pass the test of true Abrahamic sonship. "Being proved or tempted, they will *appear* to be what they have always been" (Trench).

The dominant theme of Abraham's life is that he had faith for righteousness. The Bible teaches more about faith for righteousness than about faith for anything else. But many who are specialists on the subject of faith do not give it this emphasis.

The continuous action of Abraham's faith opened channels in his life for God to do wondrous things through him, and the greatest things are still in the future.

The test of patient endurance is also stated by James (1:12). "Blessed is the man that endureth temptation, for when he is tried, he shall receive the crown of life, which the Lord hath promised to them that love him." Jesus gave an interesting contrast to this subject when He told about some who "have no root in themselves, and so endure but for a time" (lit., "they are temporary") Mark 4:17. But when tested with persecution or affliction, they fall away. The false believer endureth for a time; the true one "endureth unto the end." The faith of the false is temporary; the faith of the genuine is eternal.

The apostle Peter connected the testings of the saints to the coming of Christ, and said that out of their fiery ordeal of suffering and temptation God will get honor and praise for Christ at His coming.

> That the trial of your faith, being much more precious than of gold that perisheth, though it be tried with fire, might be found unto praise and honour and glory at the appearing of Jesus Christ.

> Beloved, think it not strange concerning the fiery trial which is to try you, as though some strange thing happened unto you.

> But rejoice, inasmuch as ye are partakers of Christ's sufferings; that, when his glory shall be revealed, ye may be glad with exceeding joy.—I Pet. 1:7; 4:12-13

Every doctrine in the Bible is related to Christ's coming. And every test of our lives is related to it. Those who will be His bride at His coming are "partakers of Christ's sufferings." Those who refuse to be partakers of His sufferings shall not be partakers of His glory. This test of sufferings also separates the true from the false.

This earth is God's proving ground for the saints. The Kingdom-people are now in the process of preparation—"to make *ready* a people prepared for the Lord." The work is done when Christ comes, not after. They come from the furnace of "manifold temptations" with imperishable faith and holiness. They are fitly represented by gold, the emblem of supreme quality and enduring beauty. They shall never perish because they loved God and obeyed His will to create within them the imperishable qualities of eternal life.

Christ and His coming was the heart of Paul's teaching. This is evident from many references in his epistles, and they show that he was ever zealous for the spiritual purity of his churches. He desired to "present" the Corinthians "as a chaste virgin to Christ.'' He told the Colossians that Christ died "to present you holy and unblameable and unreproveable in his sight.'' And he told the Thessalonians they would be his "crown of rejoicing" at Christ's coming. He also prayed for them, that, "the very God of peace sanctify you wholly; and I pray God your whole spirit and soul and body be preserved blameless unto the coming of our Lord Jesus Christ.'' Did Paul believe that his converts could so endure a life of testing that they would be holy, unblameable, and unreproveable at Christ's coming? He would not have prayed for this if he did not believe it. It is those who do not have this sanctified preparation who will "be ashamed at his coming.''

Christ, "the chief corner stone" of God's Temple, was also "a tried Stone,'' and He counsels His churches "to buy of me gold tried in the fire, that thou mayest be rich.'' Churches that are spiritually poverty-stricken would be wise to do this. It would be like a resurrection from death if they would.

The final test for the inhabited earth preceding our Lord's return is noted in Revelation 3:10:

> Because thou hast kept the word of my patience [the Gospel which requires patience to keep it], I also will keep thee from the hour of temptation, which shall come upon the whole world, to try them that dwell upon the earth.

This trial will be worldwide and extraordinary. "Here it has the article, as if '*the* temptation' were to be of no ordinary kind. 'The hour of trial' seems to be that which Christ had foretold should precede his coming'' (Pulpit Commentary). Christ promised to keep His faithful ones from this trial. Interpreters vary in their explanations about the meaning of "keep thee from the hour of temptation." Some hold it means to keep them safely through the trial. Others say it means an escape from it. The promise is specific and says they shall be kept from "the hour" of it. This seems conclusive for the latter view.

6

The Name of Jesus and the Endtime Church

God, in testing the nations, churches, and individuals, brings them face to face with the Jesus-test. Millions who appeared zealous for God turned back when they met this test. Heathen will inflict horrible torture upon their bodies, and will burn themselves to death upon an altar of fire to please God, but when missionaries preach Christ to them, instead of love for the Bridegroom, what they see is a manifestation of unbelief.

The name *Jesus* was given to Christ before His birth, and the meaning of this Name was related to His earthly mission because Gabriel said Jesus would "save his people from their sins" (Matt. 1:21). The Jesus-Name therefore is necessary for the salvation of sinners. Peter said: "Neither is there salvation in any other: for there is none other name under heaven given among men, whereby we must be saved" (Acts 4:12).

The Olivet discourse is the greatest prophetic message in the Bible, and when the apostles asked Jesus about "the sign of thy coming, and of the end of the world," one point of information He gave was: "And ye shall be hated of *all* nations for *my name's sake*" (Matt. 24:1-9). God is testing and sifting the nations today with the Jesus-test, and there is increasing hostility to this Name everywhere. It is a "sign" of His coming.

Around this Name a religious war has raged across the centuries, and it will continue until the end of the age. The greatest theological dispute of the past 20 centuries has been whether Jesus was "*a* son of God" or "*the* Son of God."

The chief cause of Jewish hatred of Jesus was not His works but His claim that He was Jesus-Messiah—the fulfillment of all the prophecies of Israel's Redeemer. Gentile hostility to the Name has been as strong as that of the Jews, and today there is widespread denial of Jesus-Savior in many Protestant denominations. In many institutions of Biblical learning, the New Testament doctrine of Jesus-God is rejected, and the graduates of these schools are no longer required to believe in the deity of Jesus to become ministers in many denominations.

Satan is mobilizing his theological forces for the endtime, and his anti-Jesus movement is farther advanced than is generally known. The present ecumenical effort to bring the religions of the world into a single union will succeed, and it is developing rapidly.

But there is a barrier to this unification, which is the Name of Jesus. This barrier must be removed —and it will be. It is being removed now. Many religions of the world believe in God but not in Jesus. The issue then is not God but Jesus. Jesus did not say His followers would be hated of all nations for the sake of God's name but for "*My* name's sake."

Jesus did not commission His church to unite the world, but foretold that, because of His name the world would be divided: "Suppose ye that I am come to give peace on earth? I tell you, Nay; but rather *division*" (Luke 12:51). These people had the mistaken opinion that Christ had come to bring peace to earth. But Jesus said He had come to bring conflict and dissension among people. The World Church peace plan and God's peace plan are in violent conflict with each other. The World Church plan is anti-Jesus and anti-Biblical.

The name of Jesus is offensive to the World Church objective because it is divisive. In public meetings of mixed religious groups, prayer is not offered in the name of Jesus because this would be objectionable to those whose membership is being sought in the world union.

Throughout the Acts of the Apostles, the Jesus-Name holds the central position of importance. The apostles were constantly holding this Name before the Jews and maintaining that Jesus was the nation's promised Messiah. This brought fierce persecution upon the apostles and they were commanded not to "speak in the name of Jesus," but they rejoiced that they were "counted worthy to suffer shame for his name" (Acts 5:40-41).

Saul of Tarsus imprisoned the early Christians who called on this Name, but at the time of his conversion, Jesus said that Paul was a chosen vessel "to bear my name before the Gentiles and kings and the children of Israel: for I will shew him how great things he must suffer for my name's sake" (Acts 9:15-16). It is the mission of the true church to bear the name of Jesus to the nations. The World Church does not do this and it is therefore a gigantic fraud. It was Paul's testimony and teaching about Jesus that made him the most persecuted man of his time. To Paul, Jesus was the center and essence of all God's revelation of truth. Jesus was to Paul what the sun is to the solar system.

Paul wrote that God has highly exalted Jesus and has "given him a name that is above every name: that at the name of Jesus every knee should bow, of things in heaven, and things in earth, and things under the earth; and that every tongue should confess that Jesus Christ is Lord, to the glory of God the Father" (Phil. 2:9-11). It is God's purpose that Jesus shall receive universal recognition. For all eternity, God has given Jesus a Name that is above "every name that is named, not only in this world, but also in that which is to come" (Eph. 1:21).

Jesus was recognized as the Christ by the demon world. When demons, fearful and screaming, were brought into His presence, they recognized Him and cried out: "Jesus, thou Son of God"; "thou art Christ the Son of God"; "the Holy One of God"; and, "they knew that he was Christ" (Matt. 8:29; Mark 1:24; Luke 4:34-41). The title "Holy One" was one of God's Old Testament names, and it is one of His various titles applied to Jesus in the New Testament.

I once heard a Mohammedan say that Mohammed had everything that Jesus had, but demons wouldn't believe that. They are not afraid of the names of Buddha or Mohammed or any other, but they tremble in terror at the name of Jesus.

Peter said that God has made Jesus "*both* Lord and Christ" (Acts 2:36). The term "Son of God" as applied to Jesus expresses His divinity and it is used more than 90 times in the New Testament. This title of deity is used of Jesus in such a sense that no other person can claim it. He who denies that Jesus is the Christ is an "antichrist." He is not only an antichrist but has made God a liar because he denies "the record that God gave of his Son" (I John 2:22; 5:10).

This Jesus-Name has been the controversy of the ages. No name has been so divisive as this Name, and it will continue to separate the world into believers and unbelievers. Strong emphasis is given to this fact in the Book of Revelation. In 12:17, Satan makes war with the true Church "which keep the commandments of God, and have the testimony of Jesus Christ." These are the two marks of identification of the genuine Church in all ages. The "blood of the Lamb" is part of the testimony of this endtime Church (12:11). In 14:12, the endtime Church "keep the commandments of God, and the faith of Jesus." This term, "the faith," appears often in the Scriptures and it expresses the entire range and content of New Testament truth, and Jesus is the Author and Finisher of it all.

In 17:6, under the symbol of a woman, John saw a world church drunken "with the blood of the martyrs of Jesus." In 20:4, he saw the endtime saints who were "beheaded for the witness of Jesus." In 19:10, the revealing angel told John he was a fellowservant of those that "have the testimony of Jesus," and that "the testimony of Jesus is the spirit of prophecy." This spirit of prophecy is a message about the return of Jesus, His defeat of Satan, and the setting up of Christ's kingdom on earth. Genuine prophetic inspiration testifies of Jesus and His final victory over all the powers of evil. All unfulfilled prophecy is concerned with this.

These texts in Revelation give us a look into the future and show what the coming conflict for the Church will be: the blood of Jesus, the testimony of Jesus, the faith of Jesus, the witness of Jesus, and the martyrs of Jesus—five marks of identification. In contrast, a major objective of the World Church is "the social and economic development of the nations"—"a world family of nations"—and, "the brotherhood of man under the Fatherhood of God."

You will not find the five marks in ecumenical objectives. The testimony, faith, witness, and blood of Jesus will be rejected by an apostate theology.

In some of the present church mergers, some pastors and congregations refuse to join because they will not be unequally yoked with others who deny that Jesus is the Christ. The remnants are increasing and they are sometimes called "The Underground Church." There will be more of these groups breaking with the world system. The deity of Christ is a mounting issue in the denominations and it looms large in the prophetic picture today.

The enemies of Jesus believed in God and claimed Him as their Father, but Jesus replied that if God were their Father they would love Him and accept His Messianic claims, but they violently rejected this. They were the leaders of the harlot church in their day and Jesus said they were an "adulterous generation." They were zealous for God but haters of Jesus. When Jesus gave sight to the man born blind, they said, "Give God the praise," but not to Jesus (John 9:24).

This hostility to Jesus was manifested for centuries before His first coming. Stephen was murdered for the same testimony that the Old Testament harlots killed the true prophets. Minutes before they smashed his head with stones, he told the 71 members of the Jewish Supreme Court:

> Ye stiffnecked and uncircumcised in heart and ears, ye do always resist the Holy Ghost: as your fathers did, so do ye.

> Which of the prophets have not your fathers persecuted? and they have slain them which shewed before of the coming of the Just One; of whom ye have been now the betrayers and murderers:

> Who have received the law by the disposition of angels, and have not kept. it.—Acts 7:51-53

World popularity is not for the Remnant Church. How can a message that brought death to prophets, Jesus, and apostles be popular today?

There were violent outbursts of hell's hatred against Jesus at His first coming and there will be much more as we approach the time for His second coming.

For years we have heard much about the God-Is-Dead teaching. But the world at large does not believe that He is dead, and Satan doesn't want them to believe that He is dead. A world belief in God is necessary to Satan's endtime purpose. Antichrist will use a world church that believes in God (Rev. 17:3, 7). A dead God would be unfavorable to Antichrist's purpose because Paul said He will sit "in the temple of God, showing himself that he is God" (II Thess. 2:4). If the world believes that God is dead, how could they accept a religious Antichrist who deceives them into believing that he is God?

Atheists did not trouble Jesus and the apostles. They did not kill Jesus. Religious men did it. The prophecies do not give us a picture of world atheism in the endtime but of a world with belief in God and unbelief in Jesus. If God were dead, those who say He is dead, and also the universe would be dead, because all things get their existence from God.

Theorists in the sciences believe that thousands of other planets in the universe are inhabited with intelligent beings, and this may be true, because as Creator, God has been in the work of creation from all eternity. And the Lordship of Jesus extends over all God's creations. No matter how many worlds may be inhabited, the relation of Jesus to the universe of beings is that of Lord and Christ, and it is only through Him that all things have their existence. All the angels worship Him (Col. 1:16-17; Heb. 1:6).

Our Lord Jesus said the Holy Spirit would glorify Him, and no man can say that Jesus is Lord (his personal Lord) but by the Holy Ghost. This revelation of Jesus will be given to all who truly desire to know that He is Christ. Without this revelation, men will only concede that He is "one of the prophets." But to all who love Him, He is Jehovah Christ.

The true church has the message of Jesus. The false church has a message that is social, economic, and materialistic. God is not indifferent to human needs, He has promised this to all who seek first the kingdom of God. Let's be true to the faith and testimony of Jesus. To unbelievers, Jesus has been the Stumbling Block of the Ages. But to those who love Him, He is the Rock of Ages.

7

God's Remnants and
the World Church

After God called Israel out of Egypt and explained His covenant purpose and objective to them, He put them through a succession of tests. Moses told them the reason for this: "For the Lord your God proveth you, to know whether ye love the Lord your God with all your heart and with all your soul" (Deut. 13:3).

The tests were severe and the qualifications high. Six hundred thousand men, beside women and children, were called out of Egypt. But when the testings were finished, "there was not left a man of them," except Joshua and Caleb because they had "wholly followed the Lord" (Ex. 12:37; Num. 26:65; 32:12). All the others had "broken the covenant" and did not enter Canaan. And God swore in His jealous wrath that they would never enter His heavenly rest (Heb. 3:11). "Many are called, but few are chosen."

For our general purpose, the word remnant signifies "a faithful minority"—"what is left after a time of testing"—"survivors from a crisis."

The history of the Bride in the Old Testament is a study of remnants. God saved these faithful minorities as a lifeline to the future. They were channels of hope—a nucleus for a new start, and through them God sent divine light across centuries of apostate darkness. The torch of truth was never extinguished

—and never shall be. In every apostate generation, the divine flame passed to another remnant.

Many times God destructively reduced the nation's population because of their covenant violations, but total destruction was never in the plan, although, as Isaiah said, the remnant is sometimes "very small." Two out of 600,000! God's people-plan sometimes seems to be in jeopardy, so much so that even a Jeremiah or Elijah sinks in despair.

The prophets wrote about the remnants. Isaiah cried out against apostate Israel but saw hope for the future in the remnants (10:21). Jeremiah was asked to pray for a remnant which was "a few of many" (42:2). Ezekiel predicted that God would send judgments of sword, famine, and pestilence upon harlot Israel but that there would be "left a remnant" (14:21-22). Joel saw a remnant in God's deliverance of Jerusalem at the time of the Apocalyptic judgments (2:32). Zephaniah wrote about the righteous character of a remnant (3:13), as also did Haggai (1:12-14).

The apostle Paul also wrote about the remnants. In showing how God's purposes could never be defeated, but accomplished in the remnants, he said:

> Isaiah also crieth concerning Israel, Though the number of the children of Israel be as the sand of the sea, a remnant shall be saved.

> For he will finish the work, and cut it short in righteousness: because a short work will the Lord make upon the earth.

> And as Isaiah said before, Except the Lord of Sabaoth had left us a seed, we had been as Sodoma, and been made like unto Gomorrha.

> God hath not cast away his people which he foreknew. Know ye not what the scripture saith of Elijah? how he maketh intercession to God against Israel, saying,

Lord, they have killed thy prophets, and digged down thine altars; and I am left alone, and they seek my life.

But what saith the answer of God unto him? I have reserved to myself seven thousand men who have not bowed the knee to the image of Baal.

Even so then at *this present time* also there is a remnant according to the election of grace.—Rom. 9:27-29; 11:2-5

God, by leaving a seed, indicated that His harvest was incomplete and will be gathered through the remnants. Each remnant is a part of the whole harvest. It is not God's will that His work be like the desolated Sodom and Gomorrah. The figurative use of the Greek word for "seed" here means: "A few survivors from whom a new generation will arise"; "a few survivors preserved as the germ of a new race." A seed contains in itself the germ of the future plant. As a farmer saves seed to begin a new planting, so also does God in all generations preserve a remnant-seed to extend His people-plan. The existence of a remnant is a sure sign that God is still working in the earth, and that He is moving toward the ultimate when all the parts will be gathered into the whole.

One day someone asked Jesus a penetrating question: "Lord are there *few* that be saved?" (Luke 13:23), and Jesus replied: "Strive [agonize] to enter in at the strait gate: for many, I say unto you, will seek to enter in, and shall not be able." This strait gate appears again in Matthew 7:14, where Jesus said: "and few there be that find it." Jesus again stressed this fact in Matthew 22:14, "For many are called but few are chosen." The comparative few are the remnant. They are also called in Scripture the "elect" and "overcomers."

Today, we see the formation of a "World Church for one world," and groups of denominations with memberships of many millions are joining this ecumenical movement. Many millions more have plans to merge with it. Emphasis is on bigness, and they boast of their numbers. Pressure for compliance with the World Church objective is being used on both ministers and laymen, and this is producing many remnants.

Some of these remnants to whom we have ministered had to submit to ecumenical authority or become part of the Remnant Church. They told us: "The ministers publicly declared that Jesus is not the Son of God, and the Bible is not the Word of God. We could tolerate it no longer. We had to get out." This crisis is worldwide today. God is sifting the churches. Both ministers and laymen must choose the World Church or the Remnant Church.

From the beginning to the end of the New Testament—through the Middle Ages—to the Reformation —to "this present time," much of church history is a record of remnants. When Jesus was born, the wise men, the shepherds, Simeon and Anna, and others were among the remnant "waiting for the consolation of Israel." The remnants are also seen in the Gospels, the Acts, and the Epistles.

From Exodus to Revelation, the story repeats itself—a minority within the majority—the quantity reduced to a quality—out of the "many," a few. Crowds followed Jesus, and multitudes were saved in the period of The Acts. But when we come to the churches in Revelation, things had changed and we see a different story.

Anyone who studies the message Christ sent to these churches will know much about what is troubling the churches today. Here we have another remnant study. The churches had been tested with false doctrines and spiritual fornication, and there had been a gradual decline in their spiritual life. Paul had dealt with these dangers in his epistles but the degenerate trend had continued until it reached a climax. Christ sent them an ultimatum. They must repent or He would execute His threatened judgments upon them.

The fornication-apostasy had spread through the Asian churches like an epidemic. Even Paul's great church at Ephesus had fallen before it, and Christ sent them a final warning:

> I know thy works, and thy labour, and thy patience, and how thou canst not bear them which are evil: and thou hast tried them which say they are apostles, and are not, and hast found them liars:
>
> And hast borne, and hast patience, and for my name's sake hast laboured, and hast not fainted.
>
> Nevertheless I have somewhat against thee, because thou hast left [forsaken] thy first love ["you no longer love Me as you did at first"—Weymouth].
>
> Remember therefore from whence thou art fallen, and repent, and do the first works; or else I will come unto thee quickly, and will remove thy candlestick out of his place, except thou repent.—Rev. 2: 2-5

A forsaken love for the things of God is the root-cause of apostasy. The favorable things Christ said about them, their works, labor, patience, hatred of evil, and what they had done for His name's sake, would not avert the impending stroke unless they repented for having abandoned their first love for Him. Their "works" were not the works of love. They were "fallen" and must return to their first love and do the works that flow from such a love. There are many religious works unacceptable to God because they are not motivated by love for Christ.

Without this love for God, everything is nothing. Paul said the same in I Corinthians 13:1-3. One may have spiritual gifts, understand all mysteries, possess all knowledge, have faith to move mountains, bestow all his goods to feed the poor, and give his body to be burned, but if he does not have this love for Christ, Paul said he is "nothing."

The grievance that Christ had against the Ephesians reminds us of Jehovah's jealousy against Israel for having deserted Him. Seeking to woo Israel back to His embrace, the offended Lover reminded them of their first love for Him: "I remember thee . . . the love of thine espousals, when thou wentest after me in the wilderness" (Jer. 2:1-3). There was a time when Israel loved the Lord but they had "played the harlot with many lovers" and refused to return.

After this refusal, one of the punishments God sent upon Israel for their persistent whoredom was this:

> Therefore the showers have been withholden, and there hath been no latter rain; and thou hadst a whore's forehead, thou refusedst to be ashamed.
> —Jer. 3:3

Everywhere today in churches of all denominations many have departed from their espousal love. This is true even in those churches that are called orthodox or fundamental. Surveys and polls report that two-thirds of those interviewed say that "Christianity is a failure." The Latter Rain has been withheld and the churches are perishing for want of a harvest.

The danger to the churches today is not from without but from the spirit of harlotry within. Professing Christians have forsaken their first love for the truth, for the prayer meeting, Bible study, and

God's work. They neglect the worship service to go off to questionable amusements or stay home to see Hollywood shows. I once pastored a church near a big race track where races were not allowed on Sundays. The managers proposed to open the track on Sundays and the local ministerial association protested. The managers chided the ministers by arguing that the people from their churches attended other sporting events on Sundays where there were similar evils. How then could they oppose the Sabbath opening of the track?

Christians spend hundreds of millions of dollars on worldly pleasures while the work of God goes begging for funds to help the needy and to take the Gospel to all the world. One of Paul's warnings for the endtime was that "in the last days perilous times shall come. For men shall be *lovers* of their ownselves . . . *lovers* of pleasures more than lovers of God" (II Tim. 3:1-4). It surely is a perilous time for the churches when there is so much self-love and pleasure-love in them. And many denominational leaders and ministers of these churches will not deal with the real cause of their problem but use carnal religious programs to keep up interest. They do not have the courage to preach against the specific sins of a forsaken love. To them that would be "negative," and they would lose money and influential members. The Latter Rain has been withheld and the sad state of the churches can be seen everywhere.

Paul, who told us more about the love of God than the other apostles, also said: "If any man love not the Lord Jesus Christ, let him be accursed [God's curse be on him—Moffatt]" (I Cor. 16:22).

The second message Christ sent to the Asian churches was to Smyrna. They were under pressure to yield to infidelity. Christ warned them that their love would be "tried," and He exhorted them to be "faithful unto death, and I will give thee a crown of life." To this church and the others, the promises were only to the overcomers. There was something in each situation to overcome, and only those found faithful in the testing would "not be hurt of the second death" (2:8-11). The remnants are the overcomers.

The third message went to Pergamos where "the doctrine of Balaam" had deceived the people into acts of prostitution as it had also led Israel into this sin. This church was orthodox in creed. Christ said they held fast to His name and "hadst not denied my faith." But their orthodoxy could not save them unless they repented of their fornication and abandoned their idols. If they did not repent, He "which hath the sharp sword with two edges" would come quickly and fight against them with it (2:12-17). What a picture! A Bridegroom with a sword!

The church at Thyatira received the fourth message. Here, as in Pergamos, there was a false teaching about God and fornication. Satan had brought the Old Testament doctrines of Balaam and Jezebel into the New Testament churches, and this seductive teaching was being tolerated in the church. There is much similar teaching even in fundamentalist churches today. Spiritual fornication is tolerated and the fornicators are allowed to remain in the churches. But Christ threatened them with spiritual death "except they repent of their deeds" (2:18-29).

Sardis was next on the list. Spiritual death had come to many and others were "ready to die." They were admonished to "hold fast, and repent." To the few who had not "defiled their [wedding] garments,"

Christ promised that He would not blot their names out of the book of life (3:1-5).

Sixth on the list was the church at Philadelphia. They had survived a crisis that left them with "a little strength." Christ promised the faithful that He would keep them from a coming worldwide temptation that would try (test) all the inhabitants of the earth (3:7-11).

The spirit of harlotry appears to have been more pernicious in the church at Laodicea than in the others. Their love for Christ was "lukewarm," and they were sunken in ease, prosperity, and false security. They were spiritually blind and naked and did not know it. They needed His eyesalve that they might see their true condition, and they must get His "white raiment" to clothe their nakedness. If they did not receive His rebuke for their half-hearted condition and repent of it, He would execute His judgment upon them (3:14-22).

The spiritual defilement that corrupted these churches is widespread today. It is unusual to find a church that is not fallen and lukewarm in their love for God and His work. Many of these fallen churches have an orthodox creed, as did the apostolic churches. They deplore those who have forsaken their orthodoxy and defected to the Ecumenicals, but they also have been defiled by the spirit of whoredom, as were the Asian churches.

Many fundamental churches tolerate a spirit of worldliness. The "mother of harlots" has her offspring everywhere, and there is no difference between the World Church and the Worldly Church if both have been corrupted by violating the Covenant of Sanctity. The punishments that fell upon the harlots in the Pergamos and Thyatira churches were similar to those that will destroy the Harlot Church.

The record of the rise and fall of spiritual movements in all church history is one of endless repetition. God raised up these movements and filled them with the Holy Spirit, and like betrothed Israel, they were "holiness unto the Lord." But Satan knew where to strike; holiness is gone and sanctification is a forgotten truth. Many ministers of fundamental churches will not have these truths preached in their churches.

Instead of getting at the real cause of their deadness, they resort to attractive programs, popular entertainment, new techniques, theatrical evangelism, prizes to increase attendance, and sermons that offend no one. All this pleases the majority but is most repulsive and sickening to Christ. May the Lord help them to see that only a return to their "first love" and "first works" can save them from a harlot's doom.

8

Faith for Christ's Coming

"When the Son of man cometh, shall he find faith on the earth?"

The one thing that God requires for anything He has is *faith*. Before it came into the language of the New Testament, the word faith had the meaning of a conviction or belief resting upon the assurance of something that had been established as certain. And it bears this sense throughout the New Testament. It is a main factor, and it holds a central place of importance in all God's dealings with mankind. It is defined in the Bible like this:

> Now faith is the substance of things hoped for, the evidence of things not seen.—Heb. 11:1

Faith then deals with the reality of unseen things that are not yet possessed. It does not need the impetus of excitement or sensation to push it onward because it wholly relies on what God is and what God said. It does not depend on appearances and feelings. The entire inner being of a faith-man enters into what God is, and his character and life are so influenced by what God has said that he moves and acts in a realm of invisible certainties.

From the origin of the word, the meaning of faith is best summed up in the word *reliance*. But it is a persuasive and steadfast reliance, not only on God's Word but what God is. "He that cometh to God must believe that he *is*." And because God *is*, all that He has said, shall *be*. Faith then, being sure of its ground, will persistently seek promised objectives —without doubting or wavering—until the heavens open. If it quits, it isn't faith.

This idea of persistent faithfulness is one of the most significant and emphasized truths in the New Testament. It reaches out and touches every part of the believer's life, and it is required as evidence of genuine faith. To fully illustrate this truth about the *continuity* of faith would require the use of many texts but we shall look at only a few. Jesus, in order to show the never-quit nature of faith and how it is necessary to be ready for His coming, told the following story:

> And he spake a parable unto them to this end, that men ought always to pray, and not to faint;
>
> Saying, There was in a city a judge, which feared not God, neither regarded man:
>
> And there was a widow in that city; and she came unto him, saying, Avenge me of mine adversary.
>
> And he would not for a while: but afterward he said within himself, Though I fear not God, nor regard man;
>
> Yet because this widow troubleth me, I will avenge her, lest by her *continual coming* she weary me.
>
> And the Lord said, Hear what the unjust judge saith.
>
> And shall not God avenge his own elect, which cry day and night unto him, though he bear long with them?
>
> I tell you that he will avenge them speedily. Nevertheless when the Son of man cometh, shall he find faith on the earth?—Luke 18:1-8

In the previous chapter Jesus was teaching about His second coming and this parable was added as a climax to that truth. This was so important to Jesus that He was continually teaching and warning the people about it.

To illustrate it, Jesus told a story about a widow who went to an unjust judge and asked for justice against an oppressor. The judge was indifferent at first but the widow's incessant pleading began to annoy him. So, to save himself from such a nuisance he gave a decision in her favor. He must get rid of this continual-coming woman.

Then Jesus applied the spiritual truth: God will vindicate His elect people, though He long delays justice for them. They must endure injustice, discouragement, persecution, and all kinds of wrong. And often they are so weary and heart-sick in the conflict that it is only by the greatest possible effort that they can continue. But their loving Lord comes and ministers to them and "they press with holy vigor on."

As we go among the churches we see many who have quit in the battle of faith. They are chronic problems to their pastors and no amount of spiritual counseling seems to help them. They sit back and look on, without the grip of faith to take hold of the things of God through prevailing prayer. They are the spasmodic kind and act according to their moods. They do not have the continual-coming spirit of the widow.

Instead of accepting God's dealings with them in faith, they are always groping and stumbling in unbelief. Their favorite question is "Why"? This why-question stops many. They cannot understand the seeming indifference of God to their needs. Why must the righteous suffer wrong when the unrighteous do not? Why does God allow the world to be filled with injustice? These are vexatious questions and unanswerable except to those with faith to accept "the *mystery* of God."

Jesus taught that the "elect" have this faith.

They know that God has wise and good reasons for all things. They reject the temptation that God is unfair and His ways unequal. This stumbling block is one of the surest devices Satan has to kill the spirit of prayer and put an end to the faith of many. Jesus knew that some would be disappointed with Him when He said: "Blessed is he, whosoever shall not be offended in me [who is repelled by nothing in me—Moffatt]."

One day an enthusiastic multitude followed Jesus and He told them about many who hear the Word of God and "immediately receive it with gladness." But He said they "have no root in themselves, and so *endure but for a time*." They have a temporary faith and soon fall away. They are excited and joyful believers, and appear to be sincere for a while. But in time of temptation and testing, their excited feelings vanish; and as the truth is not rooted in their hearts, their former habits soon seize control of them.

Thousands of professing Christians have an experience that is only in their feelings, and many unwise and unethical ministers constantly play on the carnal religious feelings of these people. It is a serious deception not to "declare the whole counsel of God" to them. They should be told that patient endurance is necessary to have faith when the Son of man cometh. "In your patience possess ye your souls [you win your souls—Moffatt]" (Luke 21:19). The endurance test is the greatest test.

The divine Author was careful to point out this particular about the constancy of faith in the Christians of the Early Church in Acts 2:42: "And they continued steadfastly in the apostles' doctrine and fellowship, and in breaking of bread, and in prayers." They were consistently loyal to the apostles' teaching, and to the prayers, fellowship, and life of the church. Being of one heart and mind with them, they were faithful both in their relation to God and men. They had inward faith and manifested the outward evidence of it—as all true believers will do.

Paul, writing to the Romans, also told about the steadfast faith of those "who by patient continuance in well doing seek for glory and honor and immortality" (Rom. 2:7). Paul here connects perseverance in doing good with immortal life. And this persistence in godliness was also taught by Jesus. The good seed falls on good ground, and are those "which in an honest and good heart, having heard the word, *keep* it, and bring forth fruit with *patience*" (Luke 8:15).

This abiding in God's Word and bringing forth the fruits of righteousness was often stressed by John the Baptist, Jesus, and the apostles. First, one must have faith that "believeth *unto* righteousness" (Rom. 10:10). Then, as Jesus taught, one must "hunger and thirst *after* righteousness." We must yearn and seek for the wholeness and completeness of all that righteousness is.

Righteousness is holiness, and Paul said that those who have been made free from sin will have "fruit unto holiness" (Rom. 6:22). This truth is frequently stated or assumed throughout the Scriptures. And it is the identifying qualification of those who have "the faith of God's elect" (Titus 1:1). The subject of divine election is never taught in the Scriptures apart from faith and righteousness.

Peter, preaching in the house of Cornelius, said that everyone that "*worketh* righteousness" is accepted by God. This is what Cornelius had done and God opened the door of salvation to him. This is what the apostle John also taught: "Ye know that every one that doeth righteousness is born of him." He said that those who live in righteousness are born of God, and those who live in sin are not. By this we can know who are "children of God," and who are "the children of the devil" (I John 3:7-10).

Looking further into this subject, we see an interesting text in I Timothy 4:16: "Take heed unto thyself, and unto the doctrine; continue in them: for in doing this, thou shalt save thyself, and them that hear thee." This is not at variance with what Paul taught in Ephesians 2:8, "For by grace are ye saved through faith; and that not of yourselves: it is the gift of God."

Paul taught both sides of this subject of salvation, and if one looks at only one side of what he taught, all he will see is a distortion and deception. God gave us one Bible which has *oneness* of truth, but many different doctrines are taught from this Bible which are a complicated mass of confusion. "God is not the author of confusion."

Far back in the Genesis period there lived a man who prophesied of Christ's second coming. His name was Enoch and he lived 365 years. A long biography could have been written about him, but all we are told is that he had faith to walk with God. And because he had faith to walk with God he had faith to be translated. Hebrews 11:5-6 says:

> By faith Enoch was translated that he should not see death; and was not found, because God had translated him: for *before* his translation he had this testimony, that he pleased God. But without faith it is impossible to please him:

It was the continuous action of Enoch's faith and righteousness that pleased God. And without such faith it is impossible to please Him. God gave testimony to Enoch before his translation. He did not have to be taken to heaven to be developed to a state of faith pleasing to God. This was done "before his translation."

The testimony that God gave of Enoch continues to be His testimony of him, and it implies that what was required for Enoch's translation is required for ours. Faith for Christ's coming isn't something that turns on and off with our feelings. A spasmodic faith can never please God.

The truth taught in these texts is the same that Jesus taught about prayer in the story of the widow. And repeated emphasis is given to this in I John 5:4, "For whatsoever is born of God overcometh the world: and this is the victory that overcometh the world, even our faith."

"Whatsoever"—meaning all that are born of God —have a faith that conquers the world. This is evidence of the new birth. An abiding faith brings lasting victory. The believer is now conquering the world because the conflict is *now*.

> *Overcometh the world.* Present active indicative of *nikao*, a continuous victory because a continuous struggle, "keeps on conquering the world" ("the sum of all the forces antagonistic to the spiritual life").
> —*Word Pictures in the New Testament,* Robertson, A. T., V. 6., p. 238, Broadman Press, Nashville, Tenn., undated.

John Wesley was quoted: "Anything that cools my love for Christ is the world."

"When the Son of man cometh, shall he find faith on the earth?" By asking this question, Jesus did not mean that there would be no faith when He comes but that He would not find much of it. What He will find will be in His "elect" people. The whole movement of their life is a successive action of faith, and they will reap the harvest of a lifetime of faith. They are like Enoch: every day of his faith-walk brought him nearer to his translation day.

The future reward is related to our present faith-fulness. May the Lord give us faith to be faithful and to "pray without ceasing." A few, like the thief crucified with Jesus, repent and are saved at the time of death. But doing all the will of God is more than just getting into the kingdom.

The prayer life of the Church has never been under greater attack than it is today, and it will continue to be so as the end draws near. Look everywhere today and see what Satan has done to the prayer life of the churches. And they think it strange that revival doesn't come!

In the story of the widow, Jesus related an unceasing spirit of intercession to His finding faith when He comes again. Indifferent and neglectful Christians should remember this and get into the battle of faith.

Many are discouraged because answers to their prayers sometimes do not come quickly. But if they never get all that they think they ought to have in this world, it will be worth a lifetime of prayer to be ready when Christ comes.

(I have written at length on this subject in my book *If Ye Continue*, published by Bethany Fellowship, Inc., Mpls., Minn.)

9

The Apostasy—
The Great One

The apostle Paul was more prophetic and wrote more about Christ's second coming in his Thessalonian epistles than in the others. His main purpose for this was to correct a false teaching about the Lord's return which had caused trouble and disorder in the church there.

False teachers said that the time for Christ's return was at hand. A deceptive "spirit" also said that Christ would immediately appear, and this had stirred up fanatical excitement. Some had quit their work and others were neglectful of their duties. Why bother about such earthly things when Christ's advent was imminent?

From Paul's day to our time there is a long and sad history to this deception. Through the centuries, many claimed to have a special revelation about the time for Christ's return and many dates were set. In recent years we have seen and heard reports over the news networks about groups of people in various parts of the world who knew the time when Christ would come. Fanatics have influenced gullible people to quit their jobs, sell their homes, dress in white robes and climb to the top of a mountain to be ready at the predicted hour. Some of these were doubtless sincere people and we feel sorry for them. But they could have saved themselves all the loss if they had believed the signs that Paul gave. "It is amazing how gullible some of the saints are when a new deceiver pulls off some stunts in religion." There are many of these stunt men everywhere today, and crowds follow them.

Paul further explained the subject to the Thessalonians and reminded them of his previous teaching that the end would not come without the appearance of certain signs. He specified that these signs must come "first." If dates were given for Christ's return, there would be no need for signs.

Even learned expositors teach that the apostles expected Christ to return in their day. But this could not have been because the apostles knew they would die before His coming (John 21:19-23). Both Peter and Paul wrote about their deaths.

To reaffirm his teaching about the time for Christ's return, Paul wrote this to the Thessalonians:

> Now we beseech you, brethren, by the coming of our Lord Jesus, and by our gathering together unto him,
>
> That ye be not soon shaken in mind, or be troubled, neither by spirit, nor by word, nor by letter as from us, as that the day of Christ is at hand.
>
> Let no man deceive you by any means: for that day shall not come, except there come a falling away *first,* and that man of sin be revealed, the son of perdition.—IIThess. 2:1-3

The sign that we are primarily concerned with here is the falling-away sign.

The Greek word for "falling away" is *apostasia,* and it signifies:

> "Abandonment,"—"giving up of one's own claim," "defection," "apostasy."—*A Greek-English Lexicon of the New Testament,* Arndt & Gingrich, p. 97, University of Chicago Press, 1957, Chicago, Ill.
>
> "Apostasia. Used absolutely, to denote the passing over to unbelief, the dissolution of the union with God

subsisting through faith in Christ."—Biblico-Theological Lexicon of the New Testament Greek. Cremer, Hermann, p. 308, London, 1895.

The coming of Christ is not intended to cause believers to be "shaken" or "troubled." That is for the unbelievers. When Jesus told about the event that Paul described, He said, "See that ye be not troubled" (Matt. 24:6). It will be a time of trouble such as the world has never seen.

There have always been apostasies, but this one will be *the* apostasy (the Greek text has the article). It will precede and prepare the way for the coming of Antichrist, and it will be the full manifestation and climax of all apostasies.

The words "rebellion" and "rejection" are also included in the definition of "falling away." Israel was an apostate nation when Christ presented Himself to them as the promised Messiah but they rejected Him. The whole history of apostasy is a record of the world's rejection of God. They then substituted their own gods and doctrines.

Of major importance to us today is the intellectual apostasy that denies Christ and His redemption. The apostles and church fathers were always refuting this heresy that was a corrupting influence in all ages. Various philosophic religious systems have perverted the plain meaning of many Scriptures that affirm the deity of Jesus. Prominent religious leaders today speak of all classes of unsaved men as being "God's children." And the truths which are the essence of Christianity have been superseded by the New Theology. They will build their own millennium of "peace and safety." They don't need Christ for that. They say the kingdom of God is not literal, but spiritual; and they want an earthly kingdom where all men can live together in a brotherhood of love, peace, security, and prosperity.

Apostasy is a defection of mind or heart—or both. In either case, it is desertion—a forsaking of God and His truth. It abandons all allegiance to God and goes its own way of self-will and unbelief.

In the Bible, the apostasies of Israel hold the center of attention. And Paul, apostle to the Gentiles, held up Israel's apostasies as a warning to the Gentile churches. Much stress is given to the lessons in these apostasies.

Israel was never wholly cured of Her spirit of desertion, and to this day she remains in blindness and unbelief. The chastisements of the captivities were remedial for a time but Her lusts of "free love" soon brought them again under the fascination of foreign lovers.

Jehovah gave to Israel a mission to the nations. She was to be His witness to the world, His exhibit of truth and glory. To her was "committed the oracles of God" and, "the glory, and the covenants, and the giving of the law, and the service of God, and the promises." She was Jehovah's queen of the earth and the crown of His shekinah glory rested upon her. Nations bowed before her and kings were her servants, but her violations of the wedding covenant caused the Bridegroom to withdraw His favors and Israel fell from her exalted position. The nation disintegrated and her servants became her masters. And Jesus foretold that the Kingdom of God would be taken from them and given to the Gentiles.

The apostasies of Israel are summed up in the prophets with the comprehensive word "fornication." This most fully expressed Her continual unfaithfulness to the Covenant. There are numerous references to this in the prophets, but no prophet so fully enlarged on the figurative sense of adultery than did

Ezekiel. No prophet so strongly indicted Israel on the charge of spiritual fornication than did Ezekiel.

Ezekiel, the prophet of symbolism, used fornication or some cognate word 20 times in the 23rd chapter of his prophecy, and there are frequent occurrences in the 16th chapter. And the frequency of this indictment with the use of these words is seen in other prophets. The words uncleanness, impurity, lewdness, filthiness, and idolatry were used in the same spiritual sense. Let's look at a few of the many references and we shall see the Biblical meaning of "falling away."

During the times of the judges, Israel would not "hearken unto their judges, but they went a whoring after other gods, and bowed themselves unto them" (Judges 2:17). This they had also done under Moses. In I Chronicles 5:25-26, Israel "went a whoring after the gods of the people of the land," and God had them bound and carried away to Assyrian captivity. In Ezekiel 6:9, we see them again in captivity because the jilted Lover said: "I am broken with their whorish heart which hath departed from me, and with their eyes, which go a whoring after their idols."

Jeremiah charged them with having "played the harlot with many lovers," and, "thou hast polluted the land with thy whoredoms" (Jer. 3:1-2). These prophets were courageous men. They didn't play politics nor seek the favor of leaders who followed the crowds. How great is the need for men with courage in the ministry today! Many are polluted with the love of money and the interests of their organizations which they have put above the interests of God. How will they answer to Him who will sit upon the judgment-seat when He comes?

Ezekiel accused the Prostitute of having "set up their idols in their hearts," and for having defiled herself with lustful political alliances with surrounding nations. "The Babylonians came to her into the bed of love, and they defiled her with their whoredom, and she was polluted with them," and because of this God said, "My mind was alienated from her" (Ezek. 23:7-18). This prophet had also told them:

> Wherefore, O harlot, hear the word of the Lord: Thus saith the Lord God; because thy filthiness was poured out, and thy nakedness discovered through thy whoredoms with thy lovers, and with all the idols of thy abominations, and by the blood of thy children, which thou didst give unto them;

> Behold, therefore, I will gather all thy lovers, with whom thou hast taken pleasure, and all them that thou hast loved, with all them that thou hast hated; I will even gather thee, and will discover thy nakedness unto them, that they may see thy nakedness.

> And I will judge thee, as women that break wedlock and shed blood are judged; and I will give thee blood in fury and jealousy.—Ezek. 16:35-38

Hosea repeated the same denunciation of Israel because of her adulterous crimes against Jehovah:

> Whoredom and wine and new wine take away the heart.

> My people ask counsel of their stocks, and their staff declareth unto them: for *the spirit of whoredoms hath caused them to err,* and they have gone a whoring from under their God.—4:11-12

> I know Ephraim, and Israel is not hid from me: for now, O Ephraim, thou committest whoredom, and Israel is defiled.

> They will not frame their doings to turn unto their God: for the spirit of whoredoms is in the midst of them, and they have not known the Lord.—5:3, 4

This spiritual sense of fornication and idolatry is brought over into the New Testament, and an example of this is in Colossians 3:5-6, where Paul said that covetousness is idolatry:

> Mortify therefore your members which are upon the earth; fornication, uncleanness, inordinate affection, evil concupiscence (unholy desire), and covetousness, which is idolatry: for which things' sake the wrath of God cometh on the children of disobedience.

Paul also dealt with the particulars of this spiritual idolatry when he wrote to the Corinthian church. He was specific with his description of Israel's apostasies and applied the warnings of this to his Gentile churches. The Corinthians were the most troublesome church that Paul had because they had tendencies and characteristics of the Israelite apostates. And the same spirit is a dominating influence in many churches today.

Paul, master teacher that he was, summed up Israel's apostasy under Moses in a few sentences. After telling how God delivered all Israel from Egypt and sustained them daily with miracles, He said;

> But with many of them God was not well pleased: for they were overthrown in the wilderness.

> Now these things were our examples, to the intent we should not lust after evil things, as they also lusted.

> Neither be ye idolaters, as were some of them; as it is written, The people sat down to eat and drink, and rose up to play.

> Neither let us commit fornication, as some of them committed, and fell in one day three and twenty thousand.—I Cor. 10:1-8

Paul twice said the Israelites were our "examples," which denotes something held up as a warning. It was their cravings to eat, drink, and play, that was at the heart of the apostasy because they had made gods of these things. These allurements to idolatry have been a favorite device with Satan in all generations. We who have been pastors for many years have pled in vain with professing Christians not to make idols of the things that God has given us the rightful use of.

Perhaps no nation has served the eat-drink-play gods more than Americans. Thousands of millions of dollars are spent every year on unnecessary things that could have been put into the work of God. How will those Christians—who are guilty of this—answer to Christ, when at His coming, they are called to settle their accounts with Him?

Jesus also mentioned these sins during the apostasies at the time of Noah and Lot, and He stressed this as much as the immoralities of those depraved nations.

> And as it was in the days of Noah, so shall it be also in days of the Son of man.
>
> They did eat, they drank, they married wives, they were given in marriage, until the day that Noah entered into the ark, and the flood came, and destroyed them all.
>
> Likewise also as it was in the days of Lot; they did eat, they drank, they bought, they sold, they planted, they builded;
>
> But the same day that Lot went out of Sodom it rained fire and brimstone from heaven, and destroyed them all.
>
> Even thus shall it be in the day when the Son of man is revealed.—Luke 17:26-30

This will be the spirit of a religious world when Christ comes. Nations will be lands of idols with shrines of lust and temples of apostasy. Satan has his churches and his ministers, and Paul said that both Satan and his ministers are "transformed as the ministers of righteousness" (II Cor. 11:15). Jesus twice told about "the synagogue of Satan" where the spiritually profane, who pretended to worship God, were worshiping Satan (Rev. 2:9; 3:9). Their place of worship was a place of harlotry—a spiritual brothel. Paul told about some of Satan's ministers when he said they "serve not our Lord Jesus Christ, but their own belly: and by good words and fair speeches deceive the hearts of the simple." Paul said these false ministers are enemies of the cross of Christ—"whose God is their belly," and, "who mind earthly things" (Phil. 3:18-19). "Crucified with Christ" is no part of their theology.

Paul went deeper into the Corinthian danger when, after the eat-drink-play admonition, he wrote:

> Ye cannot drink the cup of the Lord, and the cup of devils; ye cannot be partakers of the Lord's table, and of the table of devils.

> Do we provoke the Lord to jealousy? are we stronger than he?

Paul's reason for telling them this was because of their double-dealing with God. He said they could not divide their worship between God and the idol temples in Corinth. They were attending these idolatrous feasts and, perhaps without realizing it, they were participating in heathen fellowship with demons that were present in the temples.

Paul said he did not want them to have fellowship with demons. They could not have fellowship with Christ at the Holy Communion and have fellowship with demons at the same time. As the Holy Spirit is present at the table of the Lord, so is the spirit of Satan present at the table of demons. If they divided their worship between these two tables it would "provoke the Lord to jealousy."

It is this double-hearted dealing with God that is

offensive to Him. Moses and succeeding prophets warned the double-dealing Israelites about the disastrous consequences of this because it would arouse God's jealousy against them. At one time God told these apostates that they should be consistent and give *all* their worship and gifts to the heathen god and stop dividing them (Ezek. 20:39). "They feared the Lord, and served their own gods" (II Kings 17:33).

The apostle James also wrote about the double-minded harlots who played it two ways:

> Ye adulterers and adulteresses, know ye not that the friendship of the world is enmity with God? whosoever therefore will be a friend of the world is the enemy of God.

> Draw nigh to God, and he will draw nigh to you. Cleanse your hands, ye sinners; and purify your hearts, ye double minded.—James 4:4-9

Here again we see the repetition given to spiritual immorality. And it must have been widespread because James' epistle was written "to the twelve tribes scattered abroad" (1:1). These Jews were familiar with the Old Testament figurative use of Bridegroom-Bride, and faithful and unfaithful spouses.

Those who are friends of the world are God's enemies because they have friendship with the "god of this world" and his idols. The "world" is anything that is opposed to God and the spiritual life. The word "friendship" here includes "the idea of loving as well as being loved." Jesus also taught about this when He said:

> If the world hate you, ye know that it hated me before it hated you.

> If ye were of the world, the world would love his

own: but because ye are not of the world, but I
have chosen you out of the world, therefore the
world hateth you.—John 15:18-19

Jesus also told His enemies: "The world cannot
hate you: but me it hateth because I testify of it,
that the works thereof are evil." Any church that
bears this testimony to the world will also be hated
by it. Jesus said the Holy Spirit would testify of Him,
and that He would "reprove the world of sin, and
of righteousness, and of judgment." The Holy Spirit
has departed from many churches because they have
failed to cooperate with Him in His mission to rebuke the world for its sin and unrighteousness.

James told the double-minded they must mourn
and weep and purify their hearts because a divided
heart is unclean. The word "purify" here was used
of a sanctifying preparation before entering a place
of worship.

Everywhere in the New Testament we see this
spiritual preparation as a necessity to be ready for
Christ's coming. John was another apostle who wrote
about it:

Beloved, now are we the sons of God, and it doth not
yet appear what we shall be: but we know that, when
he shall appear, we shall be like him; for we shall
see him as he is.

And every man that hath this hope in him purifieth
himself, even as he is pure.—I John 3:2-3

The great apostasy will be the worst because it
will prepare the way for Antichrist who will use the
world church system to set up himself as the world's
god. It will be developed and prepared for him when
he comes. A religious world that crucified Christ
will accept a religious Antichrist.

To be ready for the Bridegroom we must re-
nounce the idolatrous world spirit and forsake all

idol-love. Paul said, "Flee from idolatry." He also said that "fornicators, nor idolaters, nor adulterers . . .shall inherit the kingdom of God" (I Cor. 6:9-10).

10

Remember Lot's Wife

Jesus spoke often about His second coming and He illustrated it from various sources. His mind was deeply affected by this subject and He seems to have been always thinking about it. He was continually teaching and warning the people about it. In a context about His future return, He warned: "Remember Lot's wife." Many times we have seen and heard the slogans, "Remember Pearl Harbor," "Remember the Alamo," and others, but Jesus cautioned us that we must not forget Lot's wife. There was a particular truth about this woman that Jesus wants us to remember in relation to His second coming. What then is this special lesson about her that we must not forget? In Luke 17:28-33, Jesus said:

> Likewise as it was in the days of Lot; they did eat, they drank, they bought, they sold, they planted, they builded . . . even thus shall it be in the day when the Son of man is revealed. In that day, he which shall be upon the housetop and his stuff in the house, let him not come down to take it away: and he that is in the field, let him likewise not return back.
>
> Remember Lot's wife.
>
> Whosoever shall seek to save his life shall lose it; and whosoever shall lose his life shall preserve it.

This context brings out the facts about Lot's wife. In Sodom they were buying, selling, planting and building, and had made gods of their possessions. Notice the position of "stuff in the house" in the context and its connection to Lot's wife. When we think of Sodom we usually think of their immoralities but Jesus gave it a different emphasis here. Lot's wife was not involved in the Sodomic sex wickedness.

From the analogy that Jesus drew between Sodom and the harlot world when He returns, Lot's wife represents a multitude of people who will not be ready for Him. They will perish in the coming judgments', as she perished in the destruction of Sodom —and for the same reason.

And what was this reason? Genesis 13:6, shows that Lot, like Abraham, was a wealthy man and his "substance was great." With large possessions, and caught in the spirit of the times, she had set her affections on her stuff—like the Sodomites, and she "looked back" after she had been warned not to do it. "Where your treasure is, there will your heart be also," and her treasure was in Sodom. Her possessions had become obsessions.

"Looked back" means that with an intense gazing toward Sodom, she had a yearning desire to return to her stuff. She was like the Israelites of whom Stephen said, that, "in their hearts they turned back again into Egypt." Instead of the forward faith-look toward Canaan, they looked back with fleshly desires for the things they left in Egypt. These apostates did not get back to Egypt nor did they get to Canaan. They perished in their unbelief and were buried in a place named "Graves of Lust." So also with Lot's wife. She did not get back to Sodom nor did she get to the place of safety, as her husband did. She lost both her stuff and her life.

This woman believed the angel's words about the destruction of Sodom. She was not an unbeliever or mocker like her sons-in-law, but left the city with the delivering angel who held her hand as she fled from the impending doom. She had belief but not faith. Her head was orthodox but her heart was apostate. This reminds us of Hebrews 8:9, where God said of harlot Israel: "I took them by the hand to lead them out of Egypt; [but] they continued not in my covenant, and I regarded them not, saith the Lord." God and angels can hold the hands of unbelievers but He cannot save them if they love earthly things more than Him. Jesus told us to remember Lot's wife because her love for the things of this life is the besetting sin of multitudes of professing Christians today.

Lot did not look backward to Sodom. He had the forward faith-look and saw Zoar, the city of safety. When Jesus said, "*as* it was in the days of Lot . . . *even thus* shall it be in the day when the Son of man is revealed," the force of the analogy is in the fact that "one shall be taken, and the other shall be left" —as Lot was taken to safety and his wife left for judgment. One had the look of faith, the other had the look of unbelief. A few references will show the repeated emphasis given to this in the New Testament.

In Matthew 24:50, Jesus told about the neglectful and indulgent servant who will not be prepared for His coming, and the Lord "shall come in a day when he *looketh* not for him, and in an hour that he is not aware of."

In Luke 9:62, Jesus illustrated the backward look: "No man, having put his hand to the plough, and looking back, is fit for the kingdom of God." A plowman cannot look in opposite directions at the same time. He can plow a straight furrow only as he looks ahead. Jesus said we must have a *single eye* to be "fit" for the kingdom of God (Matt. 6:22). God will have no part with a divided heart.

In II Corinthians 4:18, Paul was thinking about the same faith-look when he wrote:

> While we look not at the things which are seen, but at the things which are not seen: for the things which are seen are temporal; but the things which are not seen are eternal.

> Philippians 3:20. For our conversation [citizenship] is in heaven; from whence also we look for the Saviour, the Lord Jesus Christ.

> Titus 2:13. Looking for that blessed hope, and the glorious appearing of the great God and our Saviour Jesus Christ.

> Hebrews 9:28. So Christ was once offered to bear the sins of many; and unto them that look for him shall he appear the second time without sin unto salvation.

> Hebrews 11:10-13. By faith Abraham . . . looked for a city which hath foundations whose maker and builder is God. . . . These all died in faith, not having received the promises, but having seen them afar off, and were persuaded of them, and embraced them, and confessed that they were strangers and pilgrims on the earth.

> II Peter 3:12-14. Looking for and hasting unto [yearning for] the coming of the day of God, wherein the heavens being on fire shall be dissolved, and the elements shall melt with fervent heat.

> Nevertheless we, according to his promise, look for new heavens and a new earth, wherein dwelleth righteousness.

> Wherefore, beloved, seeing that ye look for such things, be diligent that ye may be found of him in peace, without spot and blameless.

Immediately after Jesus told about Lot's wife, He added a statement of enormous importance for entry into the kingdom of God. It is one of the spiritual laws of the kingdom, and this is how He stated it: "Remember Lot's wife. Whosoever shall seek to save his life shall lose it; and whosoever shall lose his life shall preserve it."

I think this is one of the most significant things that Jesus ever said. And in this context He warned there would be a dangerous endtime situation when a man must "not return back" to save "his stuff in the house." Today, refugees fleeing from dictators have to leave everything behind, as in Cuba and East Germany. Police have often said that in times of fire, floods, and explosions, they had to force people out of their homes to save their lives. Many have rushed back into burning homes to save their valuables and perished in the flames.

We preach these truths in our fundamental churches today but with little effect. They are so entangled in their stuff that they have no heart for those things that are necessary to be ready when Christ returns. "Having ears to hear, they hear not." I once read a story about a man who was killed because he did not hear a shout of warning. He was deaf.

On this lose-find truth about salvation, Paul wrote:

> But what things were gain to me, those I counted loss for Christ.
>
> Yea doubtless, and I count all things but loss for the excellency of the knowledge of Christ Jesus my Lord: for whom I have suffered the loss of all things, and do count them but dung, that I may *win* Christ.
>
> And be found in him, not having mine own righteousness, which is of the law, but that which is through the faith of Christ, the righteousness which is of God by faith. . . .
>
> Brethren, I count not myself to have apprehended: but this *one thing* I do, forgetting those things which are behind, and reaching forth unto those things which are before, I press [strain] toward the

mark [goal] for the prize of the high calling of God
in Christ Jesus.—Phil. 3:7-14

Three times in two verses here Paul told about
his loss that he "may win Christ," and the word
"loss" means that the things he had forsaken had
value but that he had cast them away as worthless
dung. The loss, the straining toward the goal (like
the Olympic runner), the prize, and the high calling
are all related. And they agree with what Jesus
taught about losing and finding. Paul's straining toward the goal also is in line with what Jesus said
in   Luke 13:24: "Strive [strain] to enter in at the
strait gate: for many, I say unto you, will seek to
enter in, and shall not be able."

Why is this losing and straining necessary for salvation when Paul said in Ephesians 2:8-9: "For by
grace are ye saved through faith, and that not of
yourselves: it is the gift of God: not of works, lest
any man should boast"? It is because God has made
the bestowal of His gift subject to conditions. The
warning to Lot's wife not to look back was a condition of her deliverance. She disobeyed this condition
and was lost; and this is what Jesus wants us to remember about her. If she had been willing to lose,
she would have found the city of safety.

Paul did not boast in his loss, but in winning Christ.
His loss did not save him but it was proof that he
had faith for "the righteousness of God which is by
faith." If he had not forsaken those things which he
said were "gain" to him, he would not have won
Christ.

Athletic contests was Paul's favorite illustration,
and he spoke of himself as God's athlete exerting
himself toward the heavenly Goal for "the prize
of the high calling of God in Christ Jesus." To prepare a people to be Christ's bride is indeed a high

calling and it has high qualifications.

Paul's Olympic athlete was required to take an oath, imposed by the judges, that he would comply with the rigid rules for the discipline of his body in preparation for the contest. Paul, in I Corinthians 9:24-27, wrote about this and told how he brought his body in subjection to God's laws. And as this was necessary for Paul to get the Prize, is it not also for us? Satan has deceived multitudes into believing that they will get the Prize while they continually break the rules of the contest.

In ancient sporting events, as it is today, a competitor had to first qualify to get into the contest. After this, he had to qualify to win the prize. Paul taught this, and Jesus also in Luke 9:23-25:

> And he said to them all, If any man will come after me, let him deny himself, and take up his cross daily, and follow me.

> For whosoever will save his life shall lose it: but whosoever will lose his life for my sake, the same shall save it.

> For what is a man advantaged, if he gain the whole world, and lose himself, or be *cast away?*

When Jesus turned and told the excited crowds that, to follow Him, they must forsake all, deny themselves, and take up their cross, most of them lost their enthusiasm for Him. Many were called, but few qualified to be chosen. After entering the contest, it is he who can get his cross to the Goal that will win the Prize.

Jesus taught much about "life." It was one of His favorite subjects. He said a man cannot get *life* from his wealth or possessions. He can get it only by doing the will of God. Paul said we must be free from "covetousness, which is idolatry," and that no "idolater hath any inheritance in the kingdom of Christ"

(Col. 3:5; Eph. 5:5). Jesus, in His warning about the dangers of the endtime, puts us on guard about our hearts being overcharged (overpowered) with the "cares of this life" (Luke 21:34). Christians would be wise to obey Paul in I Timothy 6:8, "And having food and raiment let us be therewith content." We have seen few of them who are content with these things.

Our materialistic age will be ripe for Antichrist and his world church. Their peace and prosperity plan will have an attractive appeal to a desperate world. And multitudes with the spirit of Lot's wife will take the bait and be caught in the trap.

Salvation is taught in the Scriptures in a present and future sense. By faith, believers now have salvation and Christ as their Savior. But in the future sense, they must be ready to meet Him when He shall "appear the second time without sin unto salvation [to make their salvation complete—Weymouth]" (Heb. 9:28).

The Olympic athlete was not crowned until he had finished the race, and Paul did not expect his crown until Christ appeared. As Paul waited for his approaching death in Rome, with the race run, and the contest won, our Lord wanted us to know what he was thinking about, so He told us:

> For I am now ready to be offered, and the time of my departure is at hand.
>
> I have fought a good fight, I have finished my course, I have kept the faith:
>
> Henceforth there is laid up for me a crown of righteousness, which the Lord, the righteous judge, shall give me at that day: and not to me only, but unto all them also that *love* his appearing.—I Tim. 4:6-8

All who love His appearing will likewise keep the faith and finish the race. We must not only look away *from* the world but look *to* Christ, as it is in Hebrews 12:1-2.

> Let us lay aside every weight, and the sin which doth so easily beset us, and let us run with patience [endurance] the race that is set before us,

> Looking unto Jesus the author and finisher of our faith, who for the joy that was set before him endured the cross, despising the shame, and is set down at the right hand of the throne of God.

Here again is the illustration of an athlete running a race for a prize. To get into the contest, we must lay aside every weight, and every besetting sin. If we do this, we then qualify to enter the race. It is a sad fact that many, who think they are running the Christian race, haven't qualified to enter the contest.

Let's remember what Jesus said about "life" in relation to Lot's wife. To her, life was earthly possessions—"stuff in the house." We meet so many like her everywhere today. To them, *life* is money, pleasure, and laying up treasures on earth. But Christ is the Life of all who are members of His Bride Church.

> When Christ, who is our life, shall appear, then shall ye also appear with him in glory.—Col. 3:4

11

How Satan Deceives
the Human Mind

There are many warnings in the Bible about deception, and the most frequent is that the human mind can be deceived. The world's history of sin and its horrible consequences began by Satan deceiving a human mind about the plain meaning of something God had said. Most of the false doctrines in Christendom today are distortions of Biblical truths.

Many of the tragedies of all church history were caused by interpreters who perverted the meaning of what "God hath said." And deceptive reasonings and teachings will continue to lead multitudes astray until the end. This is evident from Revelation 12:9, where Satan is "that old *serpent* . . . which deceiveth the whole world." The true meaning of Scripture will be an issue in the endtime world delusion. Apostate Christendom will accept the Bible but not in the sense that God gave it.

In 1964, a group of 45 Protestant and Roman Catholic scholars held an ecumenical seminar at Harvard University to discuss Biblical doctrines. The problems of interpretation were continually before these scholars and it was their opinion that "hermeneutics is crucial"; and, "hermeneutics had been at the center of the concerns of the seminar." It is also a crucial problem for many churches today that are considering ecumenical affiliation.

What are the true meanings of the Biblical terms: born again, sin, repentance, death, life, redemption, resurrection, judgment, and damnation? What does "Son of God" mean? These and other Biblical terms have been battlefields of dispute for the theologians in all ages. But the true meanings of these terms will be understood by all who, in the spirit of truth, read the Scriptures and see how they were used by Jesus and the apostles, and how they were understood by their hearers.

The history of this deception goes back to the Garden of Eden. God forbade Eve to eat of a certain tree, "lest ye die." This was a simple statement and Eve understood it, but the tempter distorted it to an opposite meaning, "Ye shall not *surely* die." Satan's strategy was to convince her that she did not have the right understanding of what God meant. And the seductive scheme was aimed at her mind with such cunning that she accepted Satan's *reasoning* about God's meaning.

Eve took the bait: God was not the kind of deity that she had conceived Him to be. Her negative concept of Him was erroneous and she needed to be set straight. He was a good God, concerned for the best interests of His creatures. There would be no penalty of death, but rather, good results would follow her act. A gracious and loving God would see to that.

When God dealt with Eve about her disobedience, she tried to evade her guilt with: "the serpent beguiled me, and I did eat" (Gen. 3:13). But this excuse was rejected and the threatened penalty of death was imposed.

Satan did not deny that God had spoken the words of commandment to Eve. He was too wise for that, but he twisted the meaning of the words. The word "beguiled" signifies that she had been deluded by a *false reasoning* about God and His words. There is a delusive reasoning about God in false doctrines. Statements of Scripture are admitted but the meaning is perverted. Paul said that God's truth is so clearly revealed that all the world will "become guilty before God" (Rom. 3:19).

Paul warned the Corinthians that they were in danger of the same seduction that deluded Eve: "But I fear, lest by any means, as the serpent beguiled Eve, so your *minds* should be corrupted from the simplicity [single-mindedness] that is in Christ" (II Cor. 11:2-3).

Paul said he had godly jealousy for them because "I have espoused you to one husband, that I may present you as a chaste virgin to Christ." But they were in danger of being enticed away from their virgin purity and becoming defiled by another teaching. The tempter's subtilty would draw them away from their espousal love for Christ without their knowing it, and they no longer would have a single-hearted love for the Bridegroom. Satan's efforts to break the bond of love between Christ and His church never ceases.

The Galatian church was another that Satan tried to cast his enchanting spell over. And Paul did not spare his rebuke when he wrote:

O foolish Galatians, who hath *bewitched* you, that ye should not obey the truth, before whose eyes Jesus Christ hath been evidently set forth, crucified among you?—Gal. 3:1-3

This "bewitched" is a strong word and it signifies "fascination," or to be brought under the spell of evil. The serpent had charmed them with false teachers who drew them away from the truth about Christ crucified, and twice Paul told them they were "foolish." It is surprising sometimes to see how foolish people can be about Bible doctrines.

With such doctrinal dangers in the apostolic churches, how much more in our time? Paul said that in the last days many would depart from the faith by listening to "seducing spirits and doctrines of devils." It is the work of these seducing spirits to entice people away from "the faith," and this term expresses the entire range and content of New Testament truth. These deceptive spirits substitute the teachings of demons for the teachings of "the Faith" (I Tim. 4:1).

Satan's efforts to defile the churches with deceptive teaching continued to the end of the apostolic age. Jesus warned His apostles about it when He told them to "take heed and beware of the leaven of the Pharisees and of the Sadducees." There was a spirit in their doctrines that was subtle and enticing, and Jesus called it "leaven," which was a symbol for false teaching that led to hypocrisy. Silent and hidden, leaven secretly works its way through the mass until the whole is leavened. It spreads from a small area at first to an all inclusive final result. The leaven of the World Church is spreading fast, and all that can be leavened, will be.

The apostle John told us about "the *spirit* of error," and there is a spirit that goes with false teaching. Eve was deceived with it. The Corinthians were in danger of becoming beguiled with it, and the Galatians had been bewitched with it. And the "doctrine of Balaam," which led to covetousness and fornication, had corrupted the Pergamos church. This leaven was also working through the prophetess Jezebel in the Thyatira church to "teach and seduce" the people to commit spiritual fornication (Rev. 2: 14-23). This spirit of error is included in what Paul said was the "mystery of iniquity," and the intent of this mysterious evil spirit is to deceive the human mind. And there will be much of it as we approach the end of the age. All kinds of delusion are coming.

In Revelation 17:2; 18:3, John said that all nations of the earth are made "drunk" by the wine of the harlot's fornication. This harlot has the world intoxicated with her *spirit* of harlotry. And in Revelation 18:23, John further explained the harlot's deception: "for by thy *sorceries* were all nations deceived." The Greek word for sorcery here is *pharmakia*. We get our word "pharmacy" from it. It signified the use of drugs, spells, charms and enchantments, and it was a word used in the magic arts.

The Harlot, with her intoxicating spirit over the world mind, will have the nations beguiled, bewitched, drunk, drugged, and under the fascination of satanic enchantment. And because they receive not "the *love* of the truth . . . God shall send them strong delusion, that they should believe a lie" (II Thess. 2:10-11). These Scriptures warn us that Satan is a dangerous enemy and that he can cast a mysterious spell over the human mind.

Paul said that false teachers are Satan's ministers, and that they are transformed into angels of light. The serpent was the first, and he completely deceived Eve with his reasoning and interpretation of God's words. In all church history, false doctrines were born when men gave non-biblical meanings to biblical language—when they threw out God's meaning and substituted their own.

Peter said that no Scripture is of "any private [personal] interpretation." A private interpretation is the personal opinion of the interpreter. It is one that its advocate cannot prove; and Paul told us to "prove all things." Satan's explanation of God's words to Eve was a private interpretation. Jesus and the apostles taught the Scriptures according to established rules of interpretation, and we look with suspicion at any teacher of Scripture who does not follow this principle.

We look now at three texts often quoted by ecumenical promoters. And we shall see how they violate the basic principles of interpretation in their application of these verses. The first is in John 17:21, where Christ prayed that His believers would be one. The second is I Corinthians 12:25, where Paul said there should be no divisions in the body of Christ. The third is Ephesians 4:5, where Paul also wrote about the unity of the Christian body.

> That they all may be one; as thou, Father, art in me, and I in thee, that they also may be one in us: that the world may believe that thou hast sent me.

> That there should be no schism in the body; but that the members should have the same care one for another.

> One Lord, one faith, one baptism.

These three verses teach the same truth, which is the unity of the body of Christ. The subject is the spiritual unity of believers in Christ, and that the spirit of this unity will make such an impression upon an unbelieving world that they will believe on Christ. Jesus said, life eternal is that they might know God, and Jesus Christ, whom God sent. Believers are chosen out of the world, and are kept from the evil of the world (John 17:3-15).

There is "one body," but it is the Body of Christ. And the unity that Christ prayed for is seen in Acts 2:1; 4:32, where "they were all in one accord," and, "the multitude of them that believed were of one heart and of one soul."

Christ and the apostles never tried to bring groups of believers and unbelievers into a single church

union. They did not seek to achieve a brotherhood
of divergent religions under the Fatherhood of God.

It is evident from the contexts of the three quoted
verses that Jesus and His apostles had no thought of
a vast earthly organization for the Church. There
isn't a hint of collective merger or external uniform-
ity. But the prophecies show that at the endtime there
will be a universal union of religions and that it will
be achieved at the sacrifice of God's truth and the
Name of Christ. Several chapters in Revelation (12-
18), show two churches at the end of the age. One
receives the drunken admiration of the world, the
other receives its drunken persecution.

There is a oneness of love and fellowship between
Christ and His Bride. Paul said that Christ is the
Head of the Body, and members of this Body also
have this oneness of love and fellowship with each
other. Paul wrote: "Be not unequally yoked together
with unbelievers," and, "come out from among them,
and be ye separate." Jesus did not pray for us to
join the peace movement in those churches where
the ministers deny that He is the Christ.

Satan is using the same method to deceive multitudes today that he used in Eden. And there will be
more of this at the endtime than ever before because
Satan has kept the worse until the last. Paul taught
that the human mind is under satanic attack when
he wrote: "And the peace of God, which passeth all
understanding, shall keep your hearts and minds
through Christ Jesus" (Phil. 4:7). The word "keep"
here means to guard or protect, and true believers
have nothing to fear.

When we love God with all our heart, soul, mind,
and strength, we can pray and believe for this protection. But a divided mind is open to deception.
"There is a way that seemeth right unto a man, but
the end thereof are the ways of death" (Prov. 14:12).

12

Christ's Coming and the World Mind

After one has studied in the fields of psychology and psychoanalysis, he comes back to the Bible with a greater appreciation of what the Bible teaches about the human mind.

There is much in the Bible that is confirmed by these sciences but there is also much that they deny. In choosing which to believe, we accept the Bible because it contains important statements about the mind that are not provable by the sciences.

To show all that the Bible teaches about the human mind would require a lengthy book, so we shall look only at a few texts that are pertinent to our subject.

The Sinai Covenant of Wedlock between God and Israel contained many promises of blessings if Israel remained faithful to the covenant, but there were also many threats and curses if they were unfaithful to it. Bodily and mental diseases were included in these curses.

Moses, in his farewell message to Israel, reminded them again and again about the covenant and urged them to be faithful to it. He spoke at length on the blessings for obedience and the curses for disobedience, and in Deuteronomy 28:28-29, he specified the mental curse:

> The Lord shall smite thee with madness, and blindness, and astonishment of heart:

> And thou shalt grope at noonday, as the blind gropeth in darkness, and thou shalt not prosper in thy ways: and thou shalt be only oppressed and spoiled evermore, and no man shall save thee.

Solomon mentioned this "madness" six times in Ecclesiastes, and he said "I applied mine heart" to investigate this madness. The word does not always mean insanity but it denotes a troubled, distracted, and unreasonable state of mind, a mental distress, a disturbing perplexity, and a derangement of the orderly mental processes. After Solomon's investigation of this matter, it was his conclusion that this abnormal state of mental disorder is related to a willful desertion of God's laws.

Perhaps Solomon read what Moses said about this and it may have helped him to arrive at his conclusion. Moses spoke again about the matter in Deuteronomy 28:65-66:

> The Lord shall give thee a trembling heart, and failing of eyes, and sorrow of mind:

> And thy life shall hang in doubt before thee; and thou shalt fear day and night, and shalt have none assurance of thy life.

Fear is one of the most prominent and most frequently mentioned subjects in the Bible. And Moses threatened Israel with a fearful and insecure life if they forsook the covenant. Specialists today, working in the field of mental disorders, continue to come up with surprising discoveries about the ruinous effects of fear on both mind and body. Fear is a basic cause of much mental trouble.

Sin is a kind of madness against God. The sinner has a hostile feeling toward God, as though God were his Adversary, because He imposed moral laws which forbid him the pleasure of his sins; and to him, God's commandments are "grievous." This hostility toward God has a deadly effect upon his body and mind. Paul tells about this in Romans 8:5-7:

> For they that are after the flesh do *mind* the things of the flesh; but they that are after the Spirit the things of the Spirit.

> For to be carnally minded is death; but to be spiritually minded is life and peace.

> Because the carnal mind is *enmity* against God: for it is not subject to the law of God, neither indeed can be.

The word "flesh" here means "corrupt human nature," and the word "enmity" denotes hate or hostility. This hate against God is now producing pernicious effects in the haters and the final result will be death. Paul said these who are in revolt against God are under the control of "the prince of the power of the air, the spirit that now worketh [operates] in the children of disobedience" (Eph. 2:2). The apostle James said that the tongue of hate is "full of deadly poison," and that "it defileth the whole body." It is a demonic evil; a satanic flame that is "set on fire of hell"—"fed with a flame from hell" (James 3:5-8, Moffatt).

Jeremiah wrote about God's judgments upon the world mind because of the world's sin and unbelief. We read in Jeremiah 25:15-18:

> For thus saith the Lord God of Israel unto me; Take the wine cup of this fury at my hand, and cause all the nations, to whom I send thee, to drink it.

> And they shall drink, and be moved, and be mad, because of the sword that I will send among them.

> Then took I the cup at the Lord's hand, and made all the nations to drink, unto whom the Lord had sent me.

In chapter 50:38, Jeremiah wrote about a people who are "mad upon their idols." And in 51:7, he wrote about the madness of the nations:

> Babylon hath been a golden cup in the Lord's hand, that made all the earth drunken: the nations have drunken of her wine; therefore the nations are mad.

This agrees with the prophecies in Revelation:

And there followed another angel, saying, Babylon is fallen, is fallen, that great city, because she made all nations drink of the wine of the wrath of her fornication.—Rev. 14:8

Come hither; I will shew unto thee the judgment of the great whore that sitteth upon many waters:

With whom the kings of the earth have committed fornication, and the inhabitants of the earth have been made drunk with the wine of her fornication. —Rev. 17:1, 2

For all nations have drunk of the wine of the wrath of her fornication, and the kings of the earth have committed fornication with her.—Rev. 18:3

Sinners must choose God's cup of blessing or His cup of jealous wrath. Those who reject Christ and His righteousness, "the same shall drink of the wine of the wrath of God, which is poured out without mixture into the cup of his indignation."

Apostasy induces a moral stupor. It is a dullness and deadness to the things of God—a moral slumber from which apostates cannot be aroused. Isaiah told the apostates in his day: "The Lord hath poured out upon you the spirit of deep sleep, and hath closed your eyes" (29:10).

Drunken harlots in a deep sleep! They have been intoxicated with a drink that stupefies the mind, impairs the reason, dethrones moral sense, and makes the conscience insensible to righteousness.

To many, there is something mystifying about the turbulence of the world mind today. Leaders are helpless in dealing with the turmoil and violence in the nations. They are trying to be optimistic, and we can understand why, but the stage is being set for Antichrist. And the present world confusion will increase in intensity until a panic-stricken world will accept Satan's christ with his supernatural solutions for the world's troubles.

We now consider two illustrations which will show the relation between sin and God's penalty upon human minds. The first is the case of Nebuchadnezzar's insanity in Daniel 4:13-37.

This powerful Oriental ruler was boastful of the greatness and splendor of his empire. While walking one day in his palace he exalted himself with pride and, forgetful of God, he boasted:

> Is not this great Babylon, that *I* have built for the house of the kingdom by the might of *my* power, and for the honor of *my* majesty?

> While the word was in the king's mouth, there fell a voice from heaven, saying, O king Nebuchadnezzar, to thee it is spoken; The kingdom is departed from thee.

> And they shall drive thee from men, and thy dwelling shall be with the beasts of the field: they shall make thee to eat grass as oxen, and seven times shall pass over thee, until thou know that the most High ruleth in the kingdom of men, and giveth it to whomsoever he will.

> The same hour was the thing fulfilled upon Nebuchadnezzar: and he was driven from men, and did eat grass as oxen, and his body was wet with the dew of heaven, till his hairs were grown like eagles' feathers, and his nails like birds' claws. (Verse 16 says: "Let his heart be changed from man's, and let a beast's heart be given unto him.")

> At the end of the days I Nebuchadnezzar lifted up mine eyes unto heaven and . . . at the same time my reason returned unto me; and for the glory of my kingdom, mine honor and brightness returned unto me . . .

> Now I Nebuchadnezzar praise and extol and honor the King of heaven, all whose works are truth, and his ways judgment: and those that walk in pride he is able to abase.—Dan. 4:30-37

This king's sin was self-idolatry. He served the idols of self-love, self-will, and self-glory. One day while he was indulging himself in self-eminence, God issued the order for a heart transplant. His human heart was taken from him and he was given the heart of a beast. Then this world ruler, like a wild maniac, with not enough sense to cut his hair and nails, roamed the forests with his animal companions. Instead of feasting at his sumptuous banquets, he ate grass as oxen.

God's penalties are first intended to bring the sinner to repentance, not to destroy him. So a merciful God withdrew the spell of madness and restored the king's reason, giving him the opportunity to repent, which he did. He was not like Pharaoh and others who hardened their hearts under the divine judgments. When the humbled king recognized God and gave Him the rightful place of worship, then God and sanity returned to the Babylonian throne.

In this case we see insanity as a direct result of sin. There are moral causes in many cases of insanity. (But we do not say it is true in *every* case.)

In thinking of Nebuchadnezzar and the abnormal mind today, we think of Paul writing about the nations that "walk in the vanity of their mind." Also, writing about the perils of the last days, he said the mass of mankind would be "highminded."

The irrational and neurotic state of the world mind today is the result of something more than natural causes. Under God's law of retribution, a self-exalted world is experiencing what Jesus said: "He that exalteth himself shall be humbled," and the descent toward depravity continues. If anyone doubts this, let him study the first chapter of Romans where Paul explained why "their foolish heart [mind] was darkened."

Jesus taught that unrepentant generations of people throw themselves open to the control of satanic spirits. Having known God's truth, if they persist in their unbelief, their "last state . . . is worse than the first"—like a spreading malignancy (Matt. 12:45). Paul said that evil men will "wax worse and worse." Peter also said that "the latter end is worse with them than the beginning." When Jesus healed the man afflicted 38 years, He warned: "Sin no more, lest a worse thing come upon thee" (John 5:14).

The diseased moral mind sinks lower and lower in the moral scale. Some go to the depths of animal nature. In some cases of insanity, the insane act like animals—like Nebuchadnezzar. David compared his enemies to wild animals. John the Baptist called the Jewish unbelievers "vipers." Jesus called them "serpents" and "swine." Paul said they were "dogs." Peter and Jude described them as "brute beasts." A savage mob, in religious hysteria, screamed at Pilate for the death of Jesus. Paul said he had "fought with beasts at Ephesus." He fought these ferocious human animals in the arena of their idolatry. The temple of the goddess Diana was in Ephesus, and "all Asia and the world" worshiped Diana. Jesus told His apostles He sent them as sheep in the midst of "wolves"—and often they were religious wolves.

The never-ending news reports of bestial crimes over the world continue to shock us. The inhuman torture of the innocent, the tidal waves of howling mob violence, and the trend toward indecent animal nakedness and sex freedom, lead us to believe that God's curse of bestiality is upon many today. "The heart of the sons of men is full of evil, and madness is in their heart while they live" (Eccles. 9:3).

The prophets, in prophetic vision, foresaw a

mental darkness descending upon the earth in the last days. Isaiah saw it and wrote: "For, behold, the darkness shall cover the earth, and gross darkness the people."

A New York scientist, working in the field of mental disorders, reported a few years ago to a United Nations committee that up to 30 percent of the world's population were suffering from some form of mental trouble. In one of the world's largest cities, a seven-year study by experts showed that four of every five in the city had some kind of mental disturbance. It will be to a world entangled in its perplexities that Antichrist will make an overwhelming appeal.

The World Church *materialistic* plan for peace and prosperity is up and coming. But how can we cooperate with such a project for a world that continues to outrage and insult God with their sins? The case of King Saul is our second illustration to show the relation between stubborn sin and God's judgment upon a human mind.

Saul had been anointed king of Israel to rule over the nation. He received his orders from God and it was of first importance that he obey the voice of the Lord. One day God commanded Saul and his army to destroy the Amalekites, a heathen tribe dwelling in a southern region. The command was specific and required the utter destruction of this enemy. But when Saul attacked the enemy he only partly obeyed God's order. "Saul and the people spared Agag, and the best of the sheep, and of the oxen, and of the fatlings, and the lambs, and all that was good" (I Sam. 15:9).

Saul, returning from the battle, met the prophet Samuel, and said to him, "Blessed be thou of the Lord: I have performed the commandment of the

Lord," but Samuel knew it was a lie. After attempting to evade his guilt, and seeing that it could not be done, he told Samuel the truth: "I feared the people, and obeyed their voice" (another leader who followed the crowd).

Saul then gave Samuel some pious talk about God and said that the forbidden spoils of war had been offered in sacrifice to God. But Samuel's rebuke was severe:

> Behold, to obey is better than sacrifice, and to hearken than the fat of rams.

> For rebellion is as the sin of witchcraft, and stubbornness is as iniquity and idolatry. Because thou hast rejected the word of the Lord, he hath rejected thee from being king.—I Sam. 15:22, 23

After this, Samuel refused to see Saul again because he perceived that he was beyond hope. Then God's judgment fell upon him: "The spirit of the Lord departed from Saul, and an evil spirit from the Lord troubled [terrified] him" (I Sam. 16:14).

Willful disobedience to God is idolatry. It is rebellion which is equally sinful with witchcraft which was punishable by death. And stubbornness is as sinful as idolatry. The same measure of evil power in one is in the other.

Saul appeared outwardly religious but inwardly he was a rebel. When confronted with his sin, he shifted the blame to the people with whom he had desired to be popular and whose wishes prevailed with him. His reasoning was deceptive and he seems not to have realized the enormity of his guilt, but God held him responsible. We have known many people who were like him.

When the Holy Spirit departed from Saul, an evil spirit seized control of his mind and he was convulsed with fits of temporary insanity. One day he was calm and contrite; another day he was a raving lunatic. One day he confessed his sin, said he played the fool, wept, repented, and then made repeated attempts to kill David. Each day the darkness deepened and the malignant spirit tightened its grip on his mind. Between each agony of torment and outburst of rage, he talked like a true penitent, but God knew he was not. He had frequent periods of sanity and insanity. The black storm clouds came and went, with intermittent rays of sunshine. But when sane, he did not turn to God, as did Nebuchadnezzar. God saw that Nebuchadnezzar was sincere in his repentance and restored him to his throne, but not Saul.

As the end drew near, Saul was in desperate need of God because the Philistines had gathered against him in great numbers. Samuel was dead, and he was forsaken of God. There was no one to go to for help. Frantic in his extremity, he went to the medium at Endor, and there he heard a message that caused him to collapse in fear.

He was told again about his sin of rebellion in refusing to obey God—"The Lord is departed from thee, and is become thine enemy . . . because thou obeyedst not the voice of the Lord" (I Sam. 26:16-18). He was also told that he and his army would be delivered into the hands of the Philistines.

When Saul went into battle against the Philistines, strange as it seems, the message he heard at Endor proved true. Saul and his sons died in battle, and his forces were defeated. He was beheaded and his body hung on the wall of Bethshan, and his enemies fastened his head in the temple of their god Dagon as a trophy of victory. Tragic end! "Saul died for his transgression which he committed against the Lord, even against the word of the Lord. . . ."

A rebellious world of sinners will likewise not escape the jealous vengeance of God, unless they repent. Saul's sin followed him wherever he went, and the effects of it haunted him until, when mortally wounded, he fell upon his sword on Mount Gilboa.

We are sad in saying that, in a long ministry, we know many in churches today who have a similar spirit of stubborn unrepentance. And they are in a serious physical, spiritual, and mental condition because of it. Nothing moves them, and no one can help them. Like Saul, there is sin in their past record that they have never made right with God and men. May the Lord yet help them to see their guilt and turn to Him with all their hearts.

We shall now look at some interesting cases of religious insanity in the New Testament. When Jesus healed the man with the withered hand in Luke 6:9-11, the Jewish leaders were filled with religious hatred at Him for curing the man on the Sabbath. Jesus tried to reason with them but it is impossible to reason with fanatics.

> Then said Jesus unto them, I will ask one thing; Is it lawful on the sabbath days to do good, or to do evil? to save life, or to destroy it?
>
> And looking round about upon them all, he said unto the man, Stretch forth thy hand. And he did so; and his hand was restored whole as the other.
>
> And they were filled with *madness;* and communed one with another what they might do to Jesus (Mark 3:6 says they plotted His death).

Dr. A. T. Robertson gained international recognition as the foremost Greek scholar of modern times, and he wrote (*Word Studies*), concerning the meaning of "madness" in this text: "Here is rage that is kin to insanity."

The Jews were wild with religious bigotry, and furious with rage because Jesus had performed an act of healing mercy to an afflicted man. They put their tradition and creed above the needs of afflicted humanity. Without conscience and reason, they were fierce in their rejection of Christ who taught it was lawful to "do good" and "save life" on the Sabbath. Such pity and love their perverted and apostate minds could not accept.

Their senseless anger led to murderous intention, and their death-plot was conceived two years before they succeeded in having Him crucified.

The above story is an example of similar events in the Gospels and Acts of the Apostles. There was something about Christ's presence in the world that had a powerful action in the sphere of men's minds. His teaching turned peaceful situations into scenes of violent agitation. Once, while teaching in His hometown, the people "wondered at the gracious words which proceeded out of his mouth," but moments later He said something that so angered them that, "filled with wrath," they rose up and tried to cast Him headlong down a hill.

The people had mistaken ideas about Christ's mission to earth, as many have today, but He corrected this with: "Think not that I am come to send peace on the earth: I am not come to send peace, but a sword" (Matt. 10:34). Christ with a sword!— and He thrust that sword deep into the heart of that "adulterous generation." This doubtless discouraged the promoters of the Peace Movement of that day.

In showing what the state of the world mind will be when Christ comes, we shall consider several statements He made about mental depravity being the result of a rejection of His truth. He said some awful things about it.

The light of the body is the eye: if therefore thine eye be single, thy whole body shall be full of light.

> But if thine eye be evil, thy whole body shall be full
> of darkness. If therefore the light that is in thee be
> darkness, how great is that darkness!—Matt. 6:22-23

Light represents God's truth, and darkness represents sin and error. When one has a single desire to
love God and do His will, his whole life shall be full
of God's light. The single-eye man has an upward
gaze and looks for Christ's appearing. But the double-
eye man tried to look in opposite directions at the
same time, but Jesus said, "No man can serve two
masters" (Matt. 6:24). The diseased eye or the eye
with a beam in it cannot see clearly. Such persons
have darkened souls. Having known the light, and
lost their singleness of purpose to love God, their
entire life has become a mass of darkness. And, the
effects of this darkness in the soul will be terrible.

Jesus spoke about the subject again in John 9:39:
"For judgment I am come into this world, that they
which see not might see; and that they which see
might be made blind."

Christ's first coming was a judgment; so also will
be His second coming. He came to blind self-righteous
men—those who claimed to be the most enlightened
men in the things of God. They had all the truth and
light they needed, and boasted that they were guides
to the spiritually blind. They were God's oracles to
the world and needed nothing from this unimpressive
Messiah. They refused to recognize the Son of God
when they saw Him, and they were judged and
blinded on the spot.

Their abiding in darkness was not only a delib-
erate choice of free will, but they loved the darkness and were "condemned *already*."

> He that believeth on him is not condemned: but he
> that believeth not is condemned already, because he
> hath not believed in the name of the only begotten
> Son of God.

And this is the condemnation that light is come into the world, and men *loved* darkness rather than light . . .

For every one that doeth evil *hateth* the light, neither cometh to the light, lest his deeds should be reproved.
—John 3:18-20

It is upon this evil heart of unbelief that God lets His sentence of blindness fall. It was upon these unbelievers that John applied Isaiah's prophecy: "He hath blinded their eyes, and hardened their heart; that they should not see with their eyes, nor understand with their heart." Jesus warned: "Walk while ye have the light, lest darkness come upon you." It is a dangerous and dreadful thing to sin against God's light.

When Jesus wept over Jerusalem, He pronounced a judgment upon the nation. They would be destroyed because they refused to receive from Him "the things which belong unto thy peace! but now are they hid from thine eyes" (Luke 19:41-44).

Here the Bridegroom wept and lamented the doom of the Harlot City. They would not have Him for their Messiah, and in doing so they were denied the peace that only He can give to a nation. We see here how Christ and peace are related. They had drunk the harlot's cup of fornication to the full. Past centuries of unfaithfulness had accumulated, and Jehovah's jealous wrath would come upon them to the uttermost. There was no hope now. Their perversity of mind had reached a deadly climax, and God's stroke of vengeance was impending.

Josephus, the Jewish historian, described the horrors that befell the Jews in the destruction of the city by the Romans in 70 A.D. He was the negotiator between the Romans and the Jews. Both he and Titus, the Roman general, pled with the Jews to surrender and save themselves from the horror that would follow if they did not. It was the desire of Titus to spare the Jews and the temple.

At least four times in the Josephus history, the "madness" and blindness of the Jews is referred to. They could not be persuaded from their insane refusal to surrender, believing that a supernatural act of God would save them. A false prophet had appeared, telling them there would be a miraculous deliverance, but this was a cruel deception.

Josephus said, "A star resembling a sword ... stood over the city." There followed one of the most horrible slaughters in all the annals of warfare. And it all happened exactly as Jesus had predicted, every detail fulfilled. (See Josephus, *Wars of the Jews,* Book V, Book VI.)

Paul, in dealing with questions about Jewish and Gentile unbelief, went into details of the subject. In Romans 1:28, he wrote:

> And even as they did not like to retain God in their knowledge, God gave them over to a reprobate mind, to do those things which are not convenient [sex perversion].

Here in Romans, Paul wrote about the decline and fall of wicked nations. Exalted in pride, they refused to have God in their knowledge, and He plunged them into the deepest depravity. It was moral disaster for them when "God gave them up to vile affections," and "gave them over to a reprobate mind" (Rom. 1:26-28).

Paul described the sexual abominations of these perverted nations and said that God abandoned them to their degeneracy. He gave them up to the cravings of their unnatural lusts, and left them hopeless in their immoral filth.

The drug and sex curse that is wild and rampaging over the earth today is God's judgment upon a Christ-rejecting world. The epidemics of sex crimes in ancient civilizations were also accompanied with the use of drugs as stimulants to passion.

A "reprobate mind" is one that God has put to the test of truth and found it worthless. When a mind passes to this state there is nothing more that God can do, and He turns it over to Satan.

Such mass perversity was a sure sign of the end of the nations in the days of Noah and Lot, and it has prophetic significance in our time. Satan's end-time plan is a global scale operation—in preparation for his presentation of Antichrist to the world.

Paul said that those who are reprobated, and sunk in the mire of their abominations, are "worthy of death" (Rom. 1:32). And well-meaning men are trying to cure this iniquity with "cultural reform"!

Paul wrote on this subject of moral blindness again in Romans 11:7-8; II Corinthians 3:14; 4:3, 4:

> Israel hath not obtained that which he seeketh for; but the election hath obtained it, and *the rest were blinded.*

> According as it is written, God hath given them the spirit of slumber [stupor], eyes that they should not see, and ears that they should not hear; unto this day.

> But their minds were blinded ... if our gospel be hid, it is hid to them that are lost: in whom the god of this world hath blinded the minds of them that believe not.

There are other texts relevant to this subject but it would be needless repetition to comment on them.

We have come a long way from Moses to Paul in showing that many Scriptures teach the same truth about God's judgment upon apostate minds. And now we come to the purpose for all we have seen. Paul, in describing the final apostasy and delusion that will open the way for Antichrist, wrote:

> And then shall the Wicked be revealed, whom the Lord shall consume with the spirit of his mouth, and shall destroy with the brightness of his coming:
>
> Even him, whose coming is after the working of Satan with all power and signs and lying wonders,
>
> And with all deceivableness of unrighteousness in them that perish; because they received not the love of the truth, that they might be saved.
>
> And for this cause God shall send them strong delusion, that they should believe a lie:
>
> That they all might be *damned* who believed not the truth, but had pleasure in unrighteousness.
> —II Thess. 2:8-12

These texts show that Antichrist's appearance on the world scene will be with "all deceivableness," and that God will send "strong delusion" upon them that receive not "the love of the truth."

The world hasn't yet seen the working of Satan in its full strength. That is reserved for the approaching end. It will be a supernatural operation with the full force of delusion on a global scale, and the result will be the apostasy of all apostasies.

God's reason for sending them delusion is because, as "they believed not the truth"—"they should believe a lie," and be damned. Under the curse of this delusion they will believe that this lie is the truth. Those whose minds are not open to truth are open to all kinds of deception. And God's sentence of condemnation is the result of their not loving the truth. An apostate world will not accept Jesus as the Christ, but they will accept Satan's "man of sin" as their Messiah. The whole Anti-Christ system is a lie. The World Church peace plan is a lie.

"For when they shall say, Peace and safety; then sudden destruction cometh upon them . . . and *they* shall not escape." Peace and prosperity is the golden text of a delusive theology. To teach that peace can come to a Christ-rejecting world is a lie. Jesus said He did not come to bring peace. How then can His church promote it? The peace plan is contrary to God's revealed Word; it clashes with the latter-day prophecies.

When Israel was hardened in their impenitence, God sent prophets to them with predictions of destruction and captivity. But false prophets also appeared among the people and prophesied that there would be no such judgment. They told the Jews they were God's chosen people and that God would not send such destruction upon His elect nation. Jeremiah said they were crying, "Peace, peace," when there is no peace. God drew His sword of vengeance, and the predicted calamities soon fell upon the nation.

Pope Paul, in the summer of 1955, came to New York and made a speech for world peace before the United Nations. His message centered around two points: peace and prosperity. It was a strong ecumenical appeal. ("Ecumenical" means the inhabited earth—that is, something worldwide in extent or influence.)

The Pope's appeal was acclaimed by no less than 107 nations and major religions that gave promises of cooperation. Immediately after the Pope's speech, a prominent Roman Catholic bishop, in a news interview, said it is the Roman Catholic purpose to bring the various world religions into one fold—the UNICHURCH.

Several months before the Pope addressed the United Nations, and also in New York, Professor Arnold Toynbee, widely called "the greatest living historian," made a statement that was announced to the world by the news channels. He said: "The time for world government has come."

The World Church and World Government will be concurrent prophetic realities. They cannot be widely separated events, and they are farther advanced now than when the Pope and Professor Toynbee spoke in 1955. The peace-prosperity plan is the most attractive offer that Satan will ever make to the nations, and a chaotic world is being conditioned for it.

The massive effort now under way for world unification will succeed. There will be a fusion of corrupt Christianity and corrupt governments. Both will be dependent upon Antichrist for support and protection and will become parts of his world system. And they will be united in a single belief and purpose. "These have *one mind*" (Rev. 17:3-13). As the true Church is "one body," so also the Harlot will be one body.

The One-World dream is on the way, and it will be brought to reality by what Paul said is "the mystery of iniquity." The word *mystery* here indicates that this satanic operation is unexplainable by any human means of intelligence. Satan's secrets are not susceptible to scientific analysis; nor can we agree with leading expositors that Satan's mysterious workings are magical tricks.

The Scriptures show that in the latter-day period Satan will work in the realm of the supernatural with demonstrations that will astonish the inhabited earth. Fascinated with Satan's messiah, all the nations will ask: "Who is like unto the beast?" "Who is able to make war with him?" (Rev. 13:3-4).

Antichrist will give the nations the kind of miracles they want. Christ's miracles did not satisfy the Jews. The healing of the sick and giving sight to the blind did not measure up to Jewish expectations of

Messiah. So they asked Him for "a sign from heaven" (Mark 8:11).

To their minds, the evidences and credentials of Messiahship would be spectacular and dazzling displays of grandeur in the celestial sphere—with flashing rays of kingdom power.

Blasphemous Jews gave Christ the title of "Beelzebub" because they said He performed miracles by this prince of demons. So, if He could show them marvels from the heavens it would put Him above suspicion of working by the power of Satan. But Jesus refused this request and said that "an evil and adulterous generation" seeketh after such a sign.

Jesus foretold that Satan and Antichrist will captivate the mind of a harlot world with "*great* signs and wonders" (Matt. 24:24). Paul said the same. The same Greek words used for the *signs* and *wonders* of Christ are used for those of Antichrist. We read in Revelation 13:13-14:

> And he doeth great wonders, so that he maketh fire come down from heaven on the earth in the sight of men.

> And deceiveth them that dwell on the earth by the means of those miracles which he had power to do.

Elijah-like, he will have power to make fire come from heaven to earth, and deceive the world. It is repeatedly stated in this chapter that power is "given" to him to do works existing outside the sphere of natural law. This indicates a supernatural source and that it is by divine permission that he does them. Such signs do not deal with the ordinary but extraordinary. As the end approaches, God and Satan will fight the greatest battle of all, and it will be warfare in the realm of the supernatural, such as mortal men have never seen.

Those who say "the days of miracles are past" may change their minds when they see Antichrist in operation. And they may then be convinced that a *natural* church is helpless against a supernatural enemy. Today, as much as at anytime in history, the Church needs to be "endued with power from on high."

A natural church is useless to God, and if the Church of Christ were only a human organization, it would have perished long ago in fiery persecutions. There were times of apostasy and oppression when only divine intervention saved it from extinction.

Antichrist will not have absolute control over everything during the endtime. God will also work on a global scale because of the large number of prophecies to be fulfilled. And this fulfillment will be by such a rapid succession of events that Jesus said it will be accomplished within the lifetime of a single generation (Luke 21:32).

When the delusion of world peace and prosperity appears to have become a reality, then God's vengeance strikes the Harlot with terrifying destruction—"then sudden destruction cometh upon them." They will then realize that they were deceived.

At Christ's second coming, the armies of the nations will mobilize to fight against Him at Armageddon, but "He that sitteth in the heavens shall laugh." David wrote that at Armageddon, the armies will "rage," but "the Lord will have them in derision" (Ps. 2:1-6).

The raging rebellion of the nations against God will continue until the very end, but God will have them in "distress" and "perplexity" (Luke 21:25), and added to this, Zechariah said that at Armageddon God will smite them with "madness" (12:1-4).

When Christ destroys the world armies "with the

brightness of his coming," an angel will descend to earth and "[cry] mightily with a strong voice, saying, Babylon the great is fallen, is fallen. . . ." Here is John's description of our Lord's coming:

> And I saw heaven opened, and behold a white horse, and he that sat upon him was called Faithful and True, and in righteousness he doth judge and make war.

> His eyes were as a flame of fire, and on his head were many crowns; and he had a name written, that no man knew, but he himself.

> And he was clothed with a vesture dipped in blood: and his name is called The Word of God.

> And the armies which were in heaven followed him upon white horses, clothed in fine linen, white and clean.

> And out of his mouth goeth a sharp sword, that with it he should smite the nations: and he shall rule them with a rod of iron: and he treadeth the winepress of the fierceness and wrath of Almighty God.

> And he had on his vesture and on his thigh a name written, KING OF KINGS, AND LORD OF LORDS.—Rev. 19:11-16

13

How We Know Prophetic Time

The Biblical prophecies have frequent mention of prophetic time or periods when prophecies will be fulfilled. The words "time" and "times" appear often in the prophecies. God has given us sufficient information about the time of Christ's return, and this knowledge is important to us. *Timing* is a deciding factor in many things. Wars have been won and lost because of it.

Christ, in His most important prophetic message, said: "Behold, I have told you *before*" (Matt. 24:25), and this advance knowledge can save us from deception. Prophetic fulfillment is preceded by signs, not dates, and all the date-setters have been wrong. A sign is a mark or indication by which a coming event is to be recognized. There is no need for a sign after the event has arrived.

The thief illustration was a favorite with Jesus. While teaching about His second coming, He said:

> Blessed are those servants, whom the lord when he cometh shall find watching . . . And this know, that if the goodman of the house had known what hour the thief would come, he would have watched, and not have suffered his house to be broken through. —Luke 12:37-39

"The day of the Lord cometh as a thief in the night" (II Pet. 3:10). The admonitions to watch indicate there will be something to see about the approaching thief. And, by watching, we can escape the danger and loss. Or, as Jesus said, the owner of the house would not have suffered his house to be broken through. So, Jesus taught here that, by watching and being prepared for the thief, you can save your life. Needless to say, it would be useless to watch after being slugged and robbed.

An illustration of watching and escaping danger is in the story (we saw before) when Jesus foretold the destruction of Jerusalem in A.D. 70 by the Romans. He wept over the city, saying:

> For the days shall come upon thee, that thine enemies shall cast a trench about thee, and compass thee round, and keep thee in on every side.
>
> And shall lay thee even with the ground, and thy children within thee; and they shall not leave in thee one stone upon another; because thou knewest not the time of thy visitation.—Luke 19:43-44

Christians cannot escape all danger, but when they have promises they can use them. The Christians escaped the Roman destruction of Jerusalem because of signs Christ had predicted. He gave military details about what the Roman General Titus would do during the siege of the city. Titus desired to save the city and the temple and for a while there were negotiations for peace. But the Christians saw the signs and knew what the result would be and fled during the early part of the siege. After one of the most horrible slaughters in all the history of war, 1,100,000 Jews were killed and 90,000 taken captive.

Dr. Alfred Edersheim, the international Jewish New Testament authority, wrote that "there can be no question" that from "these dangers the warning of the Lord delivered the Church." Dr. Edersheim cites the historians Josephus and Eusebius to show that the Christians escaped safely to Pella, on the northern boundary of Peraea. (*The Life and Times of Jesus the Messiah*, V. 2, p. 448, Wm. B. Eerdmans Co., Grand Rapids, Mich., 1953)

As we see the increasing World-Church sign today, it has serious prophetic significance. It is related to the Antichrist sign, which is also getting larger. Jesus told us to take heed to ourselves lest "that day come upon you unawares [like a trap]."

> For as a snare shall it come on all them that dwell on the face on the whole earth.

> Watch ye therefore, and pray always, that ye may be accounted worthy to escape all these things [the snare] that shall come to pass, and to stand before the Son of man.—Luke 21:35-36

To those who watch for the signs, that day shall not come unawares. They will see the trap and what it is baited with, and escape it. Why watch for it if they get caught in it?

In Hebrews 10:25, the apostle was writing about Christ's coming and said that we should exhort one another, and "so much the more, as ye see the day approaching." We do not have to wait for the full development of the signs to know the time of the Day of Christ. The point here is that we can see the approach of it. Jesus said there would be things to "see" and "hear" about His coming. When we see the trees in bud, "ye see and know of your own selves that summer is now nigh at hand." So also, when we see the signs of the kingdom, we know the kingdom is *nigh*.

There is a *law of growth* in these signs. A prophetic sign first appears and then develops by successive stages until it is full-grown—as a bud grows and ripens. Jesus said about the wheat and tares, "Let both grow together until the harvest." Also, "For the earth bringeth forth fruit of herself, first the blade, then the ear, after that the full corn in the ear." As there are successive stages of growth from seedtime to harvest, so are there connecting periods toward the completion of the Antichrist and World Church system. It will continue to develop with an increasing intensity on a worldwide scale until it reaches its maximum force. I John 2:18-20 illustrates this:

> Little children, it is the last time: and as ye have heard that antichrist shall come, even now are there many antichrists; whereby we know that it is the last time.

The apostle observed—19 centuries ago—that the antichrist sign had appeared, and he also noted the *size* of the sign, for there were "many antichrists." And he connected the sign with prophetic time: *"Whereby we know* it is the last time."

Then the apostle asked: "Who is a liar but he that denieth that Jesus is the Christ?" He who denies this is both liar and antichrist. There were many in this antichrist movement 19 centuries ago, and today there are more than ever. The World Church is swarming with antichrists.

Perhaps more than ever, this anti-Christ movement is now gathering strength as it moves toward its final stage, and it is preparing the way for *the* Antichrist. Many false prophets will consummate in *"the* false prophet" (Rev. 16:13). The "harlot" generates into "the *great* whore" (Rev. 17:1). Babylon expands into "BABYLON THE GREAT" (Rev. 17:5). Antichrist himself will also have a gradual manifestation. "He shall come up, and shall *become* strong with a small people" (Dan. 11:23). One day we were waiting at a New York airport for a friend from Europe and first saw the big plane like a speck on the horizon, but it appeared larger and larger as it approached the airport. So also shall it be as we "see the day approaching."

We note in passing that when John told about the antichrist heresy in the Church, there had been a division, and:

> They went out from us, but they were not of us; for if they had been of us, they would no doubt have *continued* with us: but they went out, that they might be made manifest that they were not all of us.—I John 2:19

Here again the Christ-test had separated the counterfeits from the genuine. John said that if they had been of the truth, they would have continued with them in the church. But they departed that their false character might be manifested. Jesus said, "If ye continue in my word, then are ye my disciples indeed." Those John told about had failed the *continue-test.* Gold can be put in the testing acid and it continues to be gold, no matter how long it remains in the acid. Counterfeits can claim what they will, but the Bible requires proof. Counterfeits can pass everything but a test.

There is something mysterious about this anti-Christ movement, and Paul speaks of it in II Thessalonians 2:7: "For the mystery of iniquity doth *already* work: only he who now hindereth will hinder, until he be taken out of the way."

Satan's world plan for the endtime is moving in secrecy, and operating by the energies of his invisible power. It is a hellish conspiracy of revolt against Christ and His Church.

Paul said this mystery was already operating in his day, and what we see today is the growth of it for 19 centuries. Advancing through the centuries, it has been picking up momemtum until today it has accumulated unprecedented force. The full power of the tornado will soon strike.

The world's masses are moving in the spirit of this mystery. President Nixon recently said, "We are living in an age of anarchy." World leaders are frustrated in trying to solve their dilemmas, and their decisions sometimes shock us. Russia is a dominant power in the world today by a mysterious chain of decisions in other governments that helped her toward this domination.

Jesus referred to this mystery-sign when He said in Matthew 24:12: "Because iniquity shall abound, the *love* of many shall grow cold." The Greek word for "abound" means that wickedness will multiply until the sum total of it fills the earth. And because of this prevailing world spirit of lawlessness, the love of many will grow cold. It is a serious fact that The Church has always been affected by the times in which it existed. How much more as the *Mystery* exerts itself for its final and uttermost effort?

The manifestation of this mystery is bringing surprising changes in the world, and to the churches. I recently heard a Protestant leader in the World Church say: "Most Protestants are now willing to accept the Pope as their spiritual leader."

We go now to I Thessalonians 5:1-3, where Paul has some important facts to tell us about prophetic time.

> But of the times and seasons, brethren, ye have no need that I write unto you.
>
> For yourselves know perfectly that the day of the Lord so cometh as a thief in the night.
>
> For when they shall say, Peace and safety; then sudden destruction cometh upon *them*, as travail upon a woman with child; and *they* shall not escape.

But *ye*, brethren, are not in darkness, that that day
should overtake *you* as a thief.

There is a time for our Lord's coming, and there
is a time for the formation of the World Church and
the coming of Antichrist. The stage must be set for
his appearance on the world scene, and certain events
will herald his approach. Paul said there are "times
and seasons" for these events.

The words "times" and "seasons" have much the
same meaning but there is a distinction. *Times* refer
to extention or duration of particular periods. It is
a span of time during which Satan has special opportunities. *Seasons* refer to shorter periods marked
with certain characteristics for prophetic growth.
The seasons come and go, leaving their fruit. Each
age has its own signs for the endtime. The final
seasons will be especially critical. There have always
been perilous times but the seasons of the last time
will be the most dangerous, as Paul wrote in
II Timothy 3:1-4: "This know also, that in the last
days perilous times shall come. For men shall be
lovers of their own selves . . . lovers of pleasures
more than lovers of God."

Times and seasons do not mean date-setting. But
from facts in the prophecies we can get an approxi-
mation. In scientific problems, if given a few facts
we can solve the problem, and God has given us sufficient information to reason to a safe conclusion.

Paul said the Thessalonians knew "perfectly" the
time when the Day of the Lord would come—as a
thief in the night. God has given us such accurate
information that, that day should not "overtake you
as a thief." The word "overtake" means "to sur-
prise and seize with hostile intent." We are admonished to "watch and pray" that we shall not be
surprised and seized with hostile intent. The word

"escape" that Paul used here is the same word that Jesus used in Luke 21:36: "Pray always, that ye may be accounted worthy to escape all these things . . ." The same word was used by Paul in II Corinthians 11:33. In Damascus, Paul's enemies were trying to kill him, but "through a window in a basket was I let down by the wall, and escaped. . . ." The word *escape* signifies "to get safely out of danger." When Paul said that "they" shall not escape the day of the Lord, the Greek text has special stress upon an emphatic negation. But we are not in darkness and have promises to escape the springing of the trap. Established rules of interpretation require this conclusion.

The Holy Spirit is trying to sound the alarm in the churches today for all who have ears to hear. But many are asleep and the thief will overtake them in their slumber. To each of the seven Asian churches in Revelation 2-3, Jesus said: "He that hath an ear, let him hear what the Spirit saith [is now saying] unto the churches."

The Holy Spirit yearns to keep us alerted and informed. Inventors are constantly working on new burglar alarm systems. One of the latest is an electronic system. When the thief enters the electronic field around the house, the alarm sounds and turns on the lights. Antichrist with all his cunning will not evade the Holy Spirit's detection.

The two signs of prophetic time that Paul gave the Thessalonians were "peace and safety." The Peace Movement is picking up support everywhere in the world today. Even Russia is interested in it. The Pope speaks often about it. The United Nations have been working on it for many years. The World Church is giving it full cooperation and is at the front of the parade carrying the peace banner. Ministerial associations in the cities of America are promoting peace, but we have declined their invitations to co-operate.

President Eisenhower returned from a European trip and told reporters: "All the world hungers for peace." A war-weary world, staggering under oppressive taxation to pay the costs of war, will accept Satan's peace plan, but it will be on his terms and at his price. Satan is bringing the nations to the brink of destruction. Military experts tell about the horrible possibility of nuclear World War III during the next few years, and they give frightful descriptions of hundreds of millions dying in the first attack. This is favorable to Satan's peace plan as he skillfully weaves his net around the world. What nation would reject a peace plan that would save the world from nuclear destruction? (President Kennedy said it would be "war that would turn this planet into a cinder.")

Any nation today that could enforce peace could control the world, but none of the superpowers can do it. Other nations have a "balance of power." But Satan will have a super miracle man who can enforce it. He will so overwhelm the nations with his military might that an astonished world will ask: "Who is able to make war with him?" The nuclear powers and all others will fall before him. He will have something this world never saw before.

The two signs Paul gave are "peace *and* safety." The two are different. *Safety* includes security or prosperity. In Papyri usage it had the sense of all-is-well. To feel secure is a basic human instinct and Satan will not overlook this. To bring peace to the world but leave the nations in poverty is not his plan. He's too wise for that. He will use the old political slogan: "Give the people what they want," and they

want peace and security. This is what the World
Church is trying to get for them. How far do you
think the World Church would get if they preached
"Christ crucified" and "holiness unto the Lord"?

Frustrated leaders of nations struggle with many
dilemmas but their problems are largely related to
peace and prosperity. The whole scope of world problems today requires extraordinary solutions. Com-
munism is a world failure. Russia and all the nations
are in money trouble, even the richest of them. They
cannot finance their welfare programs, as we see
in America today.

The prophecies show that the chaotic conditions
that will bring Antichrist are not isolated but worldwide. What Jesus called "commotions" are everywhere, and it is over this global dilemma that Antichrist casts his shadow.

Important to a knowledge of prophetic time is the
Common-Market sign. The European common
market is expanding to a world market. This will
be set up for Antichrist who will use it for his world
empire; and in the end, no man will be able to buy
or sell without his mark. The blueprints are ready
for the world market unification.

The surging economy of the European market is
attracting other nations. Those now seeking full or
partial participation are Norway, Sweden, England,
Ireland, Denmark, Greece, Turkey, African states,
and others. Even Israel has applied for membership.
This interest in the European market has led some
observers to believe that "a United States of Europe
is now on the horizon." And they are right. Twenty
years ago, France's Jean Monnet, called the "Father
of Europe," inspired the first major step toward the
creation of the Common Market and his leadership
brought it to reality in 1958. He and his collaborators

believe that a unified Europe is on the way. A recent poll of citizens of the Common Market countries showed that 65 percent favored a United States of Europe, 10 percent said "no" and 25 percent were undecided.

The 18th chapter of Revelation is a graphic picture of "great riches" spread over the earth by international shipping, or as verse 17 says, those that "trade by sea." This, together with the description of shipmasters, ships, and sailors, indicates that only a literal interpretation of this chapter agrees with the reality of the facts presented in it. The description of Babylon in verse 3 says:

> For all nations have drunk of the wine of the wrath of her fornication, and the kings of the earth have committed fornication with her, and the merchants of the earth are waxed rich through the abundance of her delicacies.

Verses 15-19 also tell about the Harlot's great riches, "wherein were made rich all that had ships in the sea by reason of her costliness."

The space given in the propheices to blocs of nations in the latter times, and to international shipping, has special interest for serious students of Biblical prophecy. And more so today when we see what is developing in the Middle East and Western Europe. The Common Market is fast emerging as an economic and monetary world power, and it is the world's most important trading unit. Europe is moving with greater unity in the Market, and this time with Britain included.

This Market now accounts for the largest bloc of international shipping, and it is the largest exporting combine in the world. America, formerly the leader in world shipping, has lost the lead and now ranks fifth. Our merchant marine is unable to challenge foreign competitors for world trade, and President Nixon recently signed a bill to begin the rebuilding of our merchant fleet at a cost of $3,000,000,000.

World trade has increased 339 percent since 1950, and maritime nations are in a race to dominate competitors in the world's markets. News reports tell about coming super cargo ships and tankers so large that shipyards in America do not have facilities to build them, so they are being built abroad. Shipping experts call this, "*The Supertransport Era.*"

Dean Rusk, former secretary of State, attended a conference in South America, and in a news conference he told about the "rapidly developing" plan for a common market in Latin America and stressed its importance to world prosperity.

The nations are seeking military and monetary security. With inflation, deflation, welfare and warfare, their money markets are frequently in danger. Smaller nations seek the protection of stronger ones. America has more than 1,000,000 of our troops stationed around the world to help others feel secure. But they have been told they can no longer.expect this help. Both America and Britain are withdrawing from further involvement in the world's problems— and when they move out, the Communists move in.

The Middle East sign is developing together with the other signs, and the countries of Daniel's image are emerging as global powers. Since the rebirth of Israel, there has been intense political and industrial activity in the nations of this image—from Iran (Persia) to Turkey, Italy, France, and from Spain to Egypt, Iraq (Babylon), and others.

Events with prophetic meaning are breaking fast on the Mediterranean scene. Military and political analysts predict a shift of world power to this area, which agrees with Revelation 18.

A great part of unfulfilled prophecy deals with the countries of Daniel's image, and Daniel was more interested in the feet of this image than in the other parts.

The center of the world common market is in this image, and vast wealth will flow from this area to all the world, as seen in Revelation 18. The center of the World Church is here. Nations once friendly to the United States now look toward Daniel's image. Daniel said the image will stand again. Dictators haven't been able to put it together but Antichrist will, and he will reign supreme with his Harlot. But their adulterous rule will be short. Daniel revealed that Christ, the Stone, will strike the Image on its 10 toes, destroy Antichrist and his kingdom, and set up His Kingdom (Dan. 2:44-45).

The Israel-sign is the most prominent, and all unfulfilled prophecy is related to it. Before His ascension, the apostles asked Jesus: "Lord, wilt thou at this *time* restore again the kingdom to Israel?" and Jesus replied: "It is not for you to know the time or the seasons which the Father hath put in his own power." But the past 25 years have been a season of phenomenal growth since the new State of Israel was established in 1948. The prophecies for Israel deal with both the people and the land. Prophecies are being fulfilled in our age that could not have been accomplished in any other, and no generation has seen the signs develop as we see them today. From a small beginning in 1948, Israel has become a power that stands against Russia and the Arab confederacy.

Our times and seasons are crucial and dangerous, and it shall be more so as we approach the end. From the few signs that we have considered, we can tell the position of the hands on God's prophetic clock.

We remember what Jesus told Judas and his mob when they came to arrest Him: "This is your hour, and the power of darkness." "To every thing there is a season, and a time to every purpose under the heaven" (Eccles. 3:1). As a physician's prognosis is based on the spread of a cancer, so by the expanding signs of the times we see the approaching end of our age.

14

Christ Speaks Seven Times From Heaven About His Return

One of the most important truths Christ taught during His earthly ministry was the certainty of His second coming. But His emphasis of this truth didn't cease with His ministry on earth. He spoke about it seven times after He ascended to heaven, indicating the great importance He attaches to this subject.

If we are wise we will heed these seven messages that Christ sent from heaven, for the Bible tells us: "See that ye refuse not him that speaketh. For if they escaped not who refused him that spake on earth [Moses], much more shall not we escape, if we turn away from him that speaketh from heaven" (Heb. 12:25).

I. The first of the seven messages was sent to the church at Thyatira. Jesus warned them, "But that which ye have already hold fast till I come" (Rev. 2:25). The reason for this warning was "because thou sufferest that woman Jezebel, which calleth herself a prophetess, to teach and seduce my servants to commit fornication, and to eat things sacrificed unto idols" (Rev. 2:20).

This symbolic language represents the spiritual fornication—or unfaithfulness to Christ—that was tolerated in the church at Thyatira under the influence of a harlot's teaching. They must reject the fornicatress and her defiling doctrine, and *hold fast* to God's high standards of spiritual purity. Satan was breaking their grip on the things of God, and they must repent and return to "the doctrine which is according to godliness" (I Tim. 6:3). This is a good rule by which we can test any teaching. Is it a doctrine according to godliness?

Jezebel, the idolatrous wife of King Ahab, was one of the most evil influences in all Israel's history. From the time of her marriage to Ahab the apostasy in Israel developed to its final stages. She was the high priestess of a corrupt religion that Jesus described as fornication.

Her seductive teaching with its deadly effect on the churches reappeared soon after the Day of Pentecost. She had long been dead, but her spirit had survived through the centuries, and had infiltrated the apostolic churches.

Many in Thyatira had come under a religious influence that left them unfaithful to their betrothal love, and the Bridegroom sent them an ultimatum. He would tolerate their harlotry no longer, and He was making a final offer of forgiveness. If they did not return to their "first [betrothal] love," He would strike them with spiritual death. We see this death everywhere in churches today. He is still the jealous Bridegroom that He was in Revelation 2:23, "And I will kill her children with death; and all the churches shall know that I am he which searcheth the reins and hearts."

One of God's Old Testament names was *Jealous*. "For thou shalt worship no other god: for the Lord, whose name is Jealous, is a jealous God" (Ex. 34:14). After Israel had persistently broken wedlock with Him and refused to repent, *Jealous* said He would give them "blood in fury and jealousy" (Ezek. 16:38), and anyone who has read the Old Testament history of God's punishments upon the Harlot will not doubt this.

Continual violations of the covenant had exhausted the patience of the Bridegroom. And on the basis of the terms established at the making of the covenant, the jealous Bridegroom carried out His threats, after all offers of mercy were rejected. It was in the spiritual sense of this retribution that Christ threatened the unfaithful in Thyatira. This law of spiritual death is still in effect, and everywhere today we see dead churches trying to stay alive with all kinds of carnal religious plans and programs that the Holy Spirit will not cooperate with.

The fornication-apostasy in the Laodicean church was even more pernicious than in the Thyatira church. They had been so completely deceived that they thought they had "need of nothing." Christ admonished them to repent of their unchastity, and as we saw before, if they did not accept His ultimatum of repentance, He would execute His threat against them.

II. Christ's second message about His coming was sent to the church at Sardis. "Remember therefore how thou hast received and heard, and hold fast and repent. If therefore thou shalt not watch, I will come on thee as a thief, and thou shalt not know what hour I will come upon thee. Thou hast a few names in Sardis which have not defiled their [wedding] garments; and they shall walk with me in white; for they are worthy" (Rev. 3:3-4).

This church was also in danger. The spirit of whoredom had defiled many and their wedding garments were polluted with impurity. Some there who were not already dead, were "ready to die," and to escape this spiritual death Christ admonished them to remember the truth they had received and heard:

to hold fast to it and repent. Like the other churches, repentance was the only hope held out to them.

This church did not need new sermons nor a sensationalist to dangle a bait to catch a crowd. Christ said they must remember the truth they had heard and to "hold fast" to it until He comes, as He also told the church at Thyatria. The same admonition is in Hebrews 2:1, "Therefore we ought to give the more earnest heed to the things which we have heard, lest at any time we should let them *slip*."

There was a dangerous crisis in this Sardis church—a turning point between life and death. If they did not repent of their defilement and cleanse their garments, Christ said He would come on them as a thief and they would not know the time of His coming.

However, there was a remnant there which had held fast to their betrothal love, and the Bridegroom promised them that they would walk with Him in eternal robes of wedlock. Although the Jezebelic spirit of impurity had worked its way into this church and turned the love of many away from Christ, a "few" had resisted this corrupting influence and retained their robes of righteousness. And Christ said they were "worthy" to walk with Him in eternal robes.

In our own works of self-righteousness we are not worthy of anything that God has. But the Scriptures teach there is a sense in which overcomers are worthy of the things of God. Jesus told about it in Matthew 10:37-39 (He also used this truth in the warning about Lot's wife):

He that loveth father or mother more than me is not worthy of me: and he that loveth son or daughter more than me is not worthy of me.

And he that taketh not his cross, and followeth after me, is not worthy of me.

He that findeth his life shall lose it: and he that loseth his life for my sake shall find it.

We see here a deep truth that Jesus repeated again and again. He is *worth* more than all earthly ties and possessions. Money, pleasure, and earthly joys are "life" to multitudes. Unless they can make the choice to *lose* this life, they cannot *find* Christ and His life. They are not worthy of Him. Eternal life is the gift of God but the conditions to be worthy of this Life were severe. Paul taught that salvation is not by works, but he also said that he had to lose all to "win Christ" and obtain the prize.

This lose-find and life-death conflict was in these Asian churches. There was death in the Sardis church as in Thyatria. To a few, Christ was worth more than all things. And Christ put an estimation of eternal value upon their love, faith, and devotion to Him. Dear reader, how much is Christ worth to you?

III. The third message was sent to the Philadelphia church. "Because thou hast kept the word of my patience, I also will keep thee from the hour of temptation, which shall come upon the whole world, to try them that dwell upon the earth. Behold, I come quickly: hold that fast which thou hast, that no man take thy crown" (Rev. 3:10-11).

The Philadelphians had kept Christ's "word of patience" which is the patient endurance that He requires for discipleship. And because they had been faithful, He promised to keep them from "the hour of temptation." They were not exempted from *all* testing; but as they had faithfully kept His word, they would be saved from the time when all nations will be put to an extraordinary test before Christ's coming.

We are told to "pray that ye enter not into temptation" (Luke 22:40). Temptations can be avoided by prayer and watching. Christ's faithful ones will not enter into this world-test because they will be watching *before it happens* and will be kept from the hour of it.

The same hold-fast warning sent to Thyatira and Sardis was sent to Philadelphia. Strong enemy powers were working in these churches to break their hold on the things of God, and three times Christ stressed the need for them to tighten their grip on the things of God.

Satan had turned his attack against the Philadelphians with such force that they were left with only a little strength. Only a small number had survived the apostasy that was testing the churches, but glorious rewards were promised to the overcomers in each situation.

IV. The fourth time Christ spoke of His coming is in Revelation 16:15: "Behold, I come as a thief. Blessed is he that watcheth, and keepeth his garments, lest he walk naked, and they see his shame." The words *watch* and *keep* are used frequently with reference to Christ's return. Here again we see the garment symbol with the heavenly warning to the churches to guard their betrothal robes. Those in the churches without these garments were spiritually naked and would suffer the shame of being exposed for what they were.

It will be spiritually indecent to appear naked before Christ at His coming. May God send us a revival of holiness!

V. The fifth reference is in Revelation 22:7. "Behold, I come quickly. Blessed is he that keepeth the sayings of the prophecy of this book."

In Revelation there is a significant recurrence of "hold fast" and "keep." The word *keep* (guard) was a favorite with Jesus during His earthly ministry and its vital meaning is expressed eight times in Revelation. The Bridegroom urges us to guard our spiritual chastity and to protect our robes of right-eousness.

VI. In Revelation 22:12, Christ spoke for the sixth time about His coming: "And, behold, I come quick-ly; and my reward is with me, to give to every man according as his work shall be."

Parts of our Lord's prophetic teaching dealt with our responsibility to His work as related to His re-turn. Those who have faith for His coming will have faith to be a "good and faithful servant." True faith manifests itself in obedience to Christ's commands about His work, but unbelief manifests itself in dis-obedience and neglect.

Jesus taught that the measure of our service to His work will be the measure of what we will re-ceive when He comes again. And Paul expressed the same thought when he said: "He which soweth sparingly shall reap also sparingly; and he which soweth bountifully shall reap also bountifully."

Viewing this truth in the light of Christ's return, we wonder why it is so difficult to get professing Christians to give themselves to the work of the Lord in their churches. The pastors plead in vain for helpers but deaf ears do not hear, and unbelieving hearts do not respond. Yet, they think they are ready for His coming. There is much idleness and neglect everywhere. The laborers are *few,* both at home and abroad. Only a few will take their share of the burden in their churches, and because of their love for His appearing, they are always "abounding in the work of the Lord." Those who do not should remember that many will "be ashamed before him at his com-ing" (I John 2:28).

VII. The last words of Christ to the Church give

us the assurance that He will come again. "He which testifieth these things saith, Surely I come quickly" (Rev. 22:20).

The curtain rises and falls in Revelation on scenes of His return, and it is Jesus, "the Amen, the faithful and true witness," who testifies to this truth. In taking the title of The Amen, Jesus guarantees both the truthfulness of the promise and the execution of it.

The writer of Hebrews said that Jesus is the "surety of a better testament." The word *surety* is a legal term, and the Biblical meaning bears the exactness of the legal sense. It eliminates doubt and uncertainty because it leaves one in a state of assurance. It confirms and guarantees because it is based on certainty.

Christ's return is guaranteed by Him as certain. We would do well to heed the apostle's warning that we shall not escape "if we turn away from him that speaketh from heaven."

15

The Final Scenes

After the destruction of Antichrist and his harlot empire, John heard a thunderous shout of praise because God had "judged the great whore, which did corrupt the earth with her fornication." The universe was exhorted to praise God for the Lamb's victory over the Babylonian fornicatress. Four times John heard their mighty "Hallelujah" and the roar of their hosannas as they fell in adoration before the Conqueror. The reason for the tumultuous rejoicing is in Revelation 19:1-9:

> *And after these things* I heard ... as it were the voice of a great multitude, and as the voice of many waters, and as the voice of mighty thunderings, saying, Alleluia: for the Lord God omnipotent reigneth.
>
> Let us be glad and rejoice, and give honour to him: for the marriage of the Lamb is come, and his wife hath made herself ready.
>
> And to her was granted that she should be arrayed in fine linen, clean and white: for the fine linen is the righteousness of saints.
>
> And he saith unto me, Write, Blessed are they which are called unto the marriage supper of the Lamb. And he saith unto me, These are the true sayings of God.

The Lamb's wedding-day is the event that all heaven is waiting for. And the marriage will be "after these things," which are the things of chapter 18, or the victory over the Harlot kingdom at Armageddon.

All that God will do in the eternal eons of time will be related to this wedding-day. As God's purposes are accomplished on earth through Christ and the Church, so also shall it be in the New Universe. The King will share all things with His Queen, and she will not only "inherit the earth," but "inherit all things" (Rev. 21:7). But "no whoremonger, nor unclean person, nor covetous man, who is an idolater, hath any inheritance in the kingdom of Christ and of God."

In the heavenly worship, much interest is on the preparation the Bride had made for her marriage. Standing beside her eternal Lover for the wedding ceremony, she is dressed in moral splendor, a marvel of holiness—a miracle of righteousness.

There's no purgatory here. The Bride had passed through that on planet earth. She had been "*chosen* . . . through sanctification of the Spirit and belief of the truth," and now she is "ready" for the marriage —as the groomsman said: "To make ready a people prepared for the Lord."

The righteous character of the Bride is described in verse 8: ". . . arrayed in fine linen, clean and white: for the fine linen is the righteousness of saints." The Greek text here reads: "the righteous *deeds* of the saints," and some translations have it like this. These are not merely good deeds or religious acts. They are not "the deeds of the law" by which self-righteous Jews hoped to be saved, but they are the actions of those who, by faith in Christ, have been brought into such a soul-saving union with God that they are obedient to all that God has declared to be *right*. These are the people who will be in the Bride of Christ.

The above text states that to the Bride it was "granted" to be clothed with the robe of righteousness, but that she had "*made herself* ready." Christ gave her the robe but she had to put it on. The spiritual meaning of putting off old garments and putting on new garments is used in both Testaments. Isaiah tried to awaken slumbering Israel with:

> Awake, awake; put on thy strength, O Zion; put on thy beautiful garments, O Jerusalem, the holy city: . . .

> Shake thyself from the dust; arise, and sit down, O Jerusalem: loose thyself from the bands of thy neck, O captive daughter of Zion.—52:1-2

Isaiah tried to get sleeping Israel to rise and shake herself loose from the dust and captivity of the world, and to put on her royal garments of moral beauty as befitting God's queen. He urged them to "put on thy strength" of spiritual loveliness, and not to trust in the strength of political alliances, money, impressive institutions, and the glorified emptiness of a religious form that was an abomination to God.

Paul used a similar metaphor in Romans 13:11-14:

> And that, knowing the time, that now it is high time to awake out of sleep: for now is our salvation nearer than when we believed.

> The night is far spent, the day is at hand: let us therefore cast off the works of darkness, and let us put on the armour of light.

> Let us walk honestly, as in the day; not in rioting and drunkenness, not in chambering and wantonness [prostitution and indecency], not in strife and envying.

> But put ye on the Lord Jesus Christ, and make not provision for the flesh, to fulfil the lusts thereof.

This put-off put-on illustration was a favorite with Paul:

Put off concerning the former conversation the old
man, which is corrupt according to the deceitful
lusts; and be renewed in the spirit of your mind;
and that ye put on the new man, which after God
is created in righteousness and true holiness.—Eph.
4:22-24

But now ye also put off all these; anger, wrath,
malice, blasphemy, filthy communication out of your
mouth. . . . Put on therefore, as the elect of God,
holy and beloved, bowels of mercies, kindness,
humbleness of mind, meekness, longsuffering.—Col.
3:8-12

But let us, who are of the day, be sober, putting on
the breastplace of faith and love; and for an helmet,
the hope of salvation.—I Thess. 5:8

"Ready" is the big word that is at the center of
all New Testament teaching about the return of
Christ. Jesus gave it repeated stress. He illustrated
it with wedding scenes, and in one parable He told
about a guest who did not have a wedding garment:

The kingdom of heaven is like a certain king, which
made a marriage for his son . . . and when the king
came in to see the guests, he saw there a man which
had not on a wedding garment:

And he saith unto him, Friend, how camest thou in
hither not having a wedding garment? And he
was speechless.

Then said the king to the servants, Bind him hand
and foot, and take him away, and cast him into
outer darkness: there shall be weeping and gnashing of teeth.

For many are called, but few are chosen.—Matt.
22:1-14

Before we try to interpret the meaning of the
wedding parables, it may help if we first lay down
a basic rule of interpretation. We must first know
the ancient Oriental marriage customs. We must look

backward over a span of 20 centuries and see the life-situation in which these parables originated, and understand them as the hearers of Jesus understood them. Without this knowledge of the ancient culture, the modern Western mind may miss the mark.

> Jesus of Nazareth was a Jew, spoke to and moved among Jews in Palestine ... He spoke first and directly to Jews, and His words must have been intelligible to them ... It was absolutely necessary to view that Life and Teaching in all its surroundings of place, society, (and) popular life.

> Even the general reader must be aware that some knowledge of Jewish life and society at the time is requisite for the understanding of the Gospel history. —*The Life and Times of Jesus the Messiah,* Edersheim, Alfred, Vol. 1, xii, xiii, Grand Rapids: Wm. B. Eerdmans Publishing Company, 1953.

> The whole Bible may be regarded as written for "the Jew first," and its words and idioms ought to be rendered according to Hebrew usage.—*Synonyms of the Old Testament—Their Bearing on Christian Doctrine,* Girdlestone, R. B., p. 14. Grand Rapids: Wm. B. Eerdmans Company, undated.

In the above parable of the marriage of the king's son, the king sent his servants to call those who were bidden to come to the wedding, but they refused. He sent other servants to tell them that the preparations for the marriage were completed and that they should come to the marriage. But "they made light of it and went their ways," which was a gross discourtesy to the king and his son. And it so angered the king that he sent his armies to destroy them and burn up their city.

Then the king told his servants to go into the highways and to invite all they met to the wedding. When all the guests had arrived, the king came in to see them, and his searching eye swept the company to see that all were properly attired. It was an *individual* inspection, and he saw one man without the required robe, and asked: "*How camest* thou in hither *not having* a wedding garment?"

The robeless guest was without excuse and was asked how he could be so disrespectful to the king by his neglectful and discourteous act.

> *Not having* on a wedding garment. It is hardly possible to convey the subtle sense of the negative particle to the English reader . . .
>
> When the king addresses the guest, he is thinking not so much of the *outward token* of disrespect, as of the guest's *mental attitude* toward the proprieties of the occasion. It is as if he had said, "What were you thinking of, where was your respect for me and my guests, when you allowed yourself to come hither *not* having the proper garment, as you knew you ought to have?" It implies . . . that the man was conscious of the omission when he entered, and was intentionally guilty of the neglect.—*Word Studies in the New Testament,* Vincent, M. R., Vol. 1, p. 120, Grand Rapids: Wm. B. Eerdmans Publishing Company, undated.

From the circumstances of the case, it is reasonable to believe that the wedding robes were given to those invited. Travelers from the highway would not have wedding robes with them. They had no thought of being invited to a wedding feast in the king's palace when they left home. Also, poor travelers, with worn and ragged clothing, would not be in proper attire to enter the king's magnificent wedding chamber, and they did not have wedding robes with them. But there was no excuse. There was a robe-room in the palace, and all they had to do was ask for the festive robe and put it on, and enjoy the wedding banquet.

Manifestly, the quickness of the invitation and the

previous unpreparedness of the guests did not prevent the procuring of such a garment. As the guests had been travellers, and as the feast was in the king's palace, we cannot be mistaken in supposing that such garments were supplied in the palace itself to all those who sought them . . .

For, although no previous state of preparedness was required of the invited guests, all being bidden, whether good or bad, yet the fact remained that, if they were to take part in the feast, they must put on a garment suited to the occasion. All are invited to the Gospel-feast; but they who will partake of it must put on the King's wedding-garment of Evangelical holiness.—Edersheim

The unrobed guest was ejected and the king's command to bind and cast him into outer darkness was executed swiftly. He was not given another opportunity to get a wedding garment. His offense to the king was beyond recall, and the sentence to outer darkness was final. The meaning of "outer darkness" is:

Hell, the place of eternal misery, confusion, and horror.—Cruden

One of the figures for hell or punishment. The repeated article makes it bolder and more impressive, "the darkness the outside," there where the wailing and gnashing of teeth is heard in the thick blackness of night.—A. T. Robertson

We come now to the parable of the virgins where Jesus warned about others who will not be "ready" for the wedding.

Then shall the kingdom of heaven be likened unto ten virgins, which took their lamps, and went forth to meet the bridegroom.

And five of them were wise, and five were foolish.

They that were foolish took their lamps, and took no oil with them:

But the wise took oil in their vessels with their lamps. While the bridegroom tarried, they all slumbered and slept.

And at midnight there was a cry made, Behold the bridegroom cometh; go ye out to meet him.

Then all those virgins arose, and trimmed their lamps. And the foolish said unto the wise, Give us of your oil; for our lamps are gone out.

But the wise answered, saying, Not so; lest there be not enough for us and you: but go ye rather to them that sell, and buy for yourselves.

And while they went to buy, the bridegroom came; and they that were *ready* went in with him to the marriage: and the door was shut.

Afterward came also the other virgins, saying, Lord, Lord, open to us.

But he answered and said, Verily I say unto you, I know you not.

Watch therefore, for ye know neither the day nor the hour wherein the Son of man cometh.—Matt. 25:1-13

An analysis of all that Jesus taught about His coming shows that preparation for it is the central truth, and this is the general purpose of these parables. Jesus did not give a point-by-point interpretation of all His parables. He sometimes gathered the meaning of an entire discourse into a single statement at the end, leaving it to be understood that this was His general intent. The interpreter who insists there is doctrinal meaning in every point in every parable may find himself confronted with insoluble difficulties. The main point then of this parable is to "watch" and be "ready" for the Bridegroom.

According to the historical custom of marriage processions, the bridegroom came from another place to be met by the bridal procession that escorted him to the place of marriage. Ten was the required number for the procession. Five of these were wise by making ample preparation to be ready—even if the bridegroom did not come at the time they thought he would. They knew he would come sometime that night but were not sure of the hour. So they took an extra-supply of oil for their lamps used in the lighted processional. It was an offense to a bridegroom if the bridesmaids were not thus prepared to meet and escort him to the place of wedding.

The folly of the foolish was their willful and careless neglect to make the necessary preparation while they had time to do it. They could not plead ignorance about the need for the oil, nor could they make excuse for not having it. And the refusal of the wise to share their extra supply with the foolish shows that "the foolish virgins could not have the consequences of their folly averted at the last moment."

As bridal virgins, it was their part of the wedding to escort the bridegroom to the bridal house, and by the neglect of previous preparation they had failed in this purpose. It will be impossible to make up for lost opportunity to prepare for the bridegroom's coming. The rush to the oil venders was in vain.

It is of no importance here, whether or not the foolish virgins finally succeeded in obtaining oil—although this seems unlikely at that time of night—since it could no longer be of any possible use, as its object was to serve in the festive procession, which was now past.

Nevertheless, and when the door was shut, those foolish virgins came, calling on the Bridegroom to open to them. But they had failed in that which could alone give them a claim to admission. Professing to be bridesmaids, they had not been in the bridal procession, and so, in truth and righteousness, He could only answer from within: "Verily I say unto you, I know you not." This not only in punishment, but in the right order of things.—Edersheim

There is no "second chance" here! Like the un-robed guest, willful carelessness had banished them from the wedding and put them beyond hope. They were unrecognized and disowned by the Bridegroom.

These foolish virgins do not represent the heathen who know not these truths, but they do represent the dry-wick believers in churches everywhere today. And all the preaching and persuasion of years has failed to open their eyes to the folly of their indifference. They are willfully blind to the truth that they must make *present* preparation for the *future* event.

If they continue to trifle away their opportunity to prepare, there will be no escape from their neglect and their folly will be beyond redemption. Christ taught this in the parables and other passages relevant to His coming, so this view is not based on the parables alone. "How shall we escape, if we neglect so great salvation?" (Heb. 2:3).

When the Bridegroom came, the wise virgins who were *ready* went with Him to the marriage, "and the door was shut." Afterward came the foolish, saying, "Lord, Lord, open to us. But he answered and said, Verily I say unto you, I know you not." Frantic in their pleading for entrance, they claimed Him as their Lord, but He said He was unable to recognize them for admittance to the wedding. "The Lord knoweth them that are his" (II Tim. 2:19).

". . . the door was shut." Various meanings have been applied to these words but, interpreted by the custom, they can have only *one* meaning, which we now consider:

The door *was shut* (ekleisthe). Effective aorist passive indicative, shut to stay shut.—*Word Pictures in the New Testament*, Robertson, A. T., V. 1, p. 198.

The *Expositors Greek Testament*, a long respected work by 17 distinguished Greek scholars, comments:

> Lord, Lord, open to us; a last, urgent, desperate appeal, knocking having preceded (Lk. 13:25) without result. The fear that they are not going to be admitted has seized their hearts.—V. 1, p. 301

> When the door is shut in this parable, there is no more entrance for any one.—*Pulpit Commentary*

Jesus again, in Luke 13:23-28, stressed the truth about the final closing of the door to the Kingdom. Here, He referred to the custom of the Jewish master who, having risen and closed the door, would not open it again:

> Then said one unto him, Lord, are there few that be saved? And he said unto them,

> Strive [struggle] to enter in at the strait gate: for many, I say unto you, will seek to enter in, and shall not be able.

> When once the master of the house is risen up, and hath shut to the door, and ye begin to stand without, and to knock at the door, saying, Lord, Lord, open to us; and he shall answer and say unto you, I know you not whence ye are:

> Then shall ye begin to say, We have eaten and drunk in thy presence, and thou hast taught in our streets.

> But he shall say, I tell you, I know not whence ye are; depart from me, all ye workers of iniquity [unrighteousness].

> There shall be weeping and gnashing of teeth, when ye shall see Abraham, and Isaac, and Jacob, and all the prophets, in the kingdom of God, and you yourselves thrust out.

This is in harmony with what Jesus taught about the foolish virgins. These also knock at a closed door and cry, "Lord, Lord, open to us," but admittance is denied. Leading New Testament authorities are

united on the meaning of this passage. Dr. Edersheim, the Jewish authority, wrote:

> It was a banquet to the friends of the King: the in-
> auguration of His Kingdom. When they found the
> door shut, they would, indeed, knock, in the confi-
> dent expectation that their claims would at once
> be recognized, and they admitted. And when the
> master of the house did not recognize them, as they
> had expected, and they reminded Him of their out-
> ward connection, He only repeated the same words
> as before, since it was not outward but inward re-
> lationship that qualified the guests.—*Life & Times,*
> V. 2, p. 300.

> The case put now is that of the master of a house
> who is giving an entertainment. He waits for a cer-
> tain time to receive his guests. At length, deeming
> that all are, or ought to be present, he rises and
> shuts the door, after which no one can be admitted.
> Some however, come later, knock at the door, and
> are refused admission.—*Expositors Greek Testa-
> ment,* V. 1, p. 568.

On the meaning of "hath shut to the door," other
Greek authorities wrote:

> Apokleio, to shut fast ... is used in Luke 13:25,
> expressing the impossibility of entrance after the
> closing.—*Expository Dictionary of New Testament
> Words,* Vine, W. E., V. 4, p. 26, London: Oliphants,
> Ltd., 1948.

> *Hath shut to* (apokleisei), first aorist active subjunc-
> tive of *apokleio* .... Note effective aorist tense and
> perfective use of *apo, slammed the door fast.—Word
> Pictures,* Robertson, A. T., V. 2, p. 190.

There is an exceeding greatness to God's love and
patience, but from the above facts it should be evident
that in God's dealings with men there comes the moment of finality. When this end is reached, privileges and opportunities are withdrawn and the des-
tinies of men are fixed forever. And when the door

to the Kingdom is closed, it will be Christ that "shutteth, and no man openeth" (Rev. 3:7). Jesus taught that to be shut out of the marriage means to be banished from the kingdom of God.

Christ gave considerable repetition to this subject as it is connected with His coming. In Matthew 25: 14-30, after telling about the virgins, He told about servants to whom He gave something to use for Him, and then went away to a far country. After a long time He returned and "reckoneth" (settled accounts) with those servants. The faithful servants were richly rewarded but the one-talent servant had been fearful and lazy, and did not use what had been entrusted to him. He also, like the unrobed guest and others, will be cast "into outer darkness." And again Jesus added the awful words, "there shall be weeping and gnashing of teeth." If they get another chance, why the weeping and gnashing?

Christ's coming will be a dreadful time of judgment for those who have been unfaithful to their high privileges. Peter said it would have been better for them not to know the truth, than to know it and be unfaithful to it. The Harlot Church, the unrobed guest, the foolish virgins, the one-talent servant, and others, are all judged and condemned when Christ comes. For four other similar cases see Matthew 8:12; 13:41-42; 24:44-51; 25:41-46. "Behold, *now* is the day of salvation." "*Today,* if ye will hear his voice, harden not your hearts."

After the judgment of Harlot-Babylon, and when "all things that offend" are cast into the eternal blackness of the outer darkness, Christ will then set up His earthly kingdom "wherein dwelleth righteousness."

The Son of man shall send forth his angels, and they

shall gather out of his kingdom all things that offend, and them which do iniquity:

And shall cast them into a furnace of fire: there shall be wailing and gnashing of teeth.

Then shall the *righteous* shine forth as the sun in the kingdom of their Father. Who hath ears to hear, let him hear.—Matt. 13:41-43; 25:31-46

The Book of Revelation closes with a description of the new Jerusalem, the "water of life," and the "tree of life." It leaves us with much that is unrevealed about the eternal future, but what is revealed is glorious:

And I John saw the holy city, new Jerusalem, coming down from God out of heaven, prepared as a bride for her husband.

And I heard a great voice out of heaven saying, Behold, the tabernacle of God is with men, and he will dwell with them, and they shall be his people, and God himself shall be with them, and be their God . . .

And he that sat upon the throne said, Behold, I make all things new. And he said unto me, Write: for these words are true and faithful.—Rev. 21:2-5

The Creator will create a new universe—an eternal one. The present universe, although billions of years old, was intended to be temporary—". . . the heavens are the works of thy hands: they shall perish; but thou remainest; and they all shall wax old as doth a garment: and as a vesture shalt thou fold them up, and they shall be changed" (Heb. 1:10-12). But the new Kingdom-universe will be eternal. God will create "new heavens" as well as a new earth.

This new Kingdom, multiplying and perpetually increasing forever, will have no limits to its extent in the new universe. "Of the *increase* of his government and peace there shall be *no end*" (Isa. 9:7). Christ and His Bride will be the reigning King and Queen over this ever-expanding Kingdom in the new universe, and the New Jerusalem—the Wedding-City —will be the center and capital of this new creation.

Job, Solomon, and Paul believed there is much about God and His purposes that is unknowable. Newton, Einstein, and other intellectual giants also believed this about the physical universe.

But from the Scriptures, we know that, in the movement of God's purposes through the eons of eternal time, it was His desire to get a bride for His Son. The greater part of this purpose has been completed. The remainder will soon follow.

The vastness and wonder of this subject overwhelms the imagination. Our brief outline of it could be expanded into volumes, but we think the reader has seen enough to know why God took about 15 centuries to write a Book and ended it all with the description of a wedding.

John, in closing his prophecy, wrote:

> Blessed are they that do his commandments, that they may have right to the tree of life, and may enter in through the gates into the city.

> For without are dogs, and sorcerers, and whoremongers, and murderers, and idolaters, and whosoever loveth and maketh a lie.

> I Jesus have sent mine angel to testify unto you these things *in the churches.* I am the root and the offspring of David, and the bright and morning star.

> And the Spirit and the bride say, Come. And let him that heareth say, Come. And let him that is athirst come. And whosoever will, let him take the water of life freely.

All those now on earth who love His appearing, live in the joyful expectation of hearing the heavenly announcement: "Behold, the Bridegroom cometh!" And they join in the prayer of the saints of the ages:

> Amen, Even so, come, Lord Jesus. The grace of our Lord Jesus Christ be with you all. Amen.